The CHESHIRE Cook Book

with Taste Cheshire.
A celebration of the amazing food & drink on our doorstep.
Featuring over 50 stunning recipes.

The Cheshire Cook Book

©2016 Meze Publishing. All rights reserved.

First edition printed in 2016 in the UK.

ISBN: 978-1-910863-07-7

*Thank you to: Simon Radley, Stephen Wundke and
all at Taste Cheshire for their support,
David & Julie Mitchell the Chester Town Criers
and all at The Clink.*

Compiled by: Anna Tebble

Written by: Kate Eddison

Photography by:
Marc Barker (www.marcabarker.com)
Tim Green (www.timgreenphotographer.co.uk)

Edited by: Rachel Heward, Phil Turner

Designed by: Paul Cocker, Marc Barker

Cover art: Luke Prest, www.lukeprest.com

*Contributors: Kelsie Marsden, Faye Bailey,
Georgia Tingle, Sarah Koriba, Kerre Chen,
Emily Beaumont*

Published by Meze Publishing Limited
Unit 1 Beehive Works
Milton Street
Sheffield S3 7WL
Web: www.mezepublishing.co.uk
Tel: 0114 275 7709
Email: info@mezepublishing.co.uk

CONTENTS

FOREWORD

At the tender age of 22, my career at the much acclaimed Chester Grosvenor began. Little did I know, as an aspirational young novice, that I would still be rattling pans there nearly three decades later.

My privileged position as Executive Chef has enabled me to source the finest ingredients from an abundance of expert growers and producers both near and far. For me, true satisfaction is derived from discovering such exemplary produce worldwide and especially on your doorstep.

Cheshire is that doorstep. Its bounty of pasture and plain gives rise to a plethora of stunning ingredients and enables us to support both British farmers and producers, whilst satisfying our customers' desire for provenance.

World-famous cheeses, rare-breed meat, the freshest fruits and seasonal vegetables can all be sourced from within the county, and this book is a celebration of all the people who farm, grow, make, cook and promote them. Mostly, it's a celebration of the people who choose to go out and buy them, who support local producers and enjoy everything the county has to offer.

Cheshire's larder inspires.

Take advantage.

Simon Radley

Taste CHESHIRE

Taste Cheshire is the definitive website for food and drink in Cheshire.

Taste Cheshire was created four years ago to connect food-loving people with a real "Taste of Cheshire", whether it's the best independently run restaurants, that superb local pub that goes out of its way to offer home-cooked food sourced from local suppliers, outstanding food and drink festivals (of which our county has more than any other!) or the wealth of incredible local producers and farm shops that dot the county. And proudly, that's what we do.

To be listed on the Taste Cheshire website, you must be a member of either the Restaurant Association of Cheshire (if you are a venue that sells food and drink for consumption on or off the premises) or a member of Made in Cheshire (which says you create very special food and drink flavours in Cheshire). Our Patron is His Grace, The Duke of Westminster and we are proud of our association with a family who believe so strongly in the county and the food and drink it produces.

Our natural produce is world-renowned and rooted in history. Cheshire cheese, Britain's oldest named cheese, dates back to Roman Britain and gets a special mention in the Domesday Book of 1086. In the 16th century, Cheshire cheese was reputed to be the best cheese in Europe and was a favourite at the Court of Elizabeth I – that's some pedigree! To this day,

our Cheesemakers cherish their heritage and their immense artisan skills. Did you know the largest cheese competition in the world takes place at Nantwich in Cheshire every July? We are proudly one of the judges at this incredible event.

Another familiar favourite is Mornflake. Milling oats in the South Cheshire countryside since 1675, they are the longest established miller of oats and cereal in the UK. We boast popcorn-makers, gin distillers, 46 micro-breweries, the best Chinese vegetables available outside China thanks to Dennis Ford, amazing pork pies and so much more.

You'll find a superb choice of places to eat and drink, from a Michelin-starred restaurant to idyllic country inns throughout the region. The Chester Grosvenor is one of only four restaurants in the UK to have been awarded their Michelin star consecutively for over 25 years. In addition, it is one of only a small number of restaurants in the UK to be awarded 4 AA Rosettes.

We also have an array of young guns who are producing outstanding foods as Chef Du Patrons – just take a look at The Chef's Table in Chester for example. With so many foodie destinations to visit, this website is the definitive guide to Cheshire food and drink. Explore, enjoy and bon appetit!

The Chester Food, Drink &
LIFESTYLE FESTIVAL

Chester Racecourse at Easter is the setting for what is now the biggest event of its type anywhere in the UK.

The Chester Food, Drink and Lifestyle Festival features an incredible line-up of chefs and food celebrities, headlined by people like Sunday Brunch star Simon Rimmer, MasterChef supremo Gregg Wallace and Lancashire chef sensation Andrew Nutter, as well as some of the region's finest chefs such as Dave Mooney, Luke Thomas, Sean Wilson and Brian Mellor. The chefs are complemented by over 150 food and drink producers who occupy the centre of the racecourse with huge inside and outside areas with plenty of seating for eating and drinking.

Crowds are regularly in the region of 30,000, according to Principal Organiser Stephen Wundke: "Our event has just grown and grown over the years and it is wonderful to see so many families out having a brilliant day enjoying food and drink together. I don't know of any other event where, for less than £20, a family can have 4-5 hours being entertained and enjoying some of the best food and drink on display anywhere, so it easy to see why this event has become so popular with North West families."

Over the years this event has become much more than just a food and drink festival. Alongside the free chef demonstrations and children's cooking workshops (over 900 children got involved in 2015!), Camperfest welcomes 450 caravans, motor homes and tents and offers the opportunity for families to enjoy a "staycation" at the festival. Three years ago saw the creation and addition of ArtFest, where 40 artists and galleries show a huge array of visual art and free daily seminars from artists. It's inclusive and accessible, so it's art for all this Easter.

The Chester Food and Drink Festival reaches out beyond just the three days of Easter, with the CH1 Chester BID, Sous Chef Challenge. This is a chance for chefs from Chester, below the level of Head Chef, to compete and be judged on the stage by MasterChef supremo, Gregg Wallace. There is also the annual sausage competition where butchers compete to be crowned the "Taste Cheshire Sausage of the Festival" – the winner goes on to compete for the UK "Champion of Champions" title in October.

Attached to the festival are the Taste Cheshire Food and Drink Awards. These awards are the definitive hospitality awards voted for by the public and then judged by industry experts. Here they find the best restaurants, pubs, cafés, sandwich bars, those who excel at customer service and child-friendly venues. In 2015 a record 20,000 votes were cast and you can enter your favourite Cheshire venue for free, simply by going to the festival website and voting.

There is so much going on, but all the information is contained within the website, including a 25% discount if you buy your tickets online. Children under 12 are free and so is your parking – it's just a brilliant day out!

www.chesterfoodanddrink.co.uk

ALLINGTON
HUGHES

Law

Cyfraith
Allington Hughes
Law

Chester   01244 312166
Wrexham 01978 291000
Llanrwst 01492 641222

Taste Cheshire MARKETS

Cheshire is blessed with a number of market towns that still provide an opportunity for our all-important small food and drink producers to sell their wares.

Every month the producers of Made in Cheshire line up at two feature farmers markets to sell some of the best locally produced ingredients.

The first farmers market happens on the second Friday of each month in the car park of the Grosvenor Garden Centre on Wrexham Road in Rossett. This is a terrific setting with the added bonus of being in one of the premier Garden Centres in the UK, right on the edge of the Duke of Westminster's estate. In addition to the market once a month, the Grosvenor Garden Centre also has a Taste Cheshire retail area within the shop where you can buy many Made in Cheshire goods every day of the week – so you can stock up on your local favourites between farmers markets! However the market is a great opportunity to see all the producers together, buy goods directly and talk to the people who make them. There is so much pride and passion for local produce, it's the perfect place to learn about things grown and made in the county. This market runs from 9.00am until 2.00pm.

The second market happens on the third Saturday of each month in Town Hall Square, Chester. Almost 30 different producers set up from 9.30 in the morning through until 4.00pm in the shadows of Chester Cathedral. It's a brilliant setting and the day is most often accompanied by the sounds of a steel band who create a wonderful atmosphere as people try pies, olives, bread, award-winning sausages, smoked salmon, pickled onions, biltong, cheese and many other amazing flavours.

It's always a great day and after 3 years of this important Chester market, traders now have regular customers who look for them each month to stock up on their products.

Local farmers markets are an important part of the small producers' route to market and such a great way for food lovers to find a regular supply of wonderful and unique tastes. For more information about these two markets, and of course many more that happen right across the county, go to the website, where dates and times of key markets are listed.

www.tastecheshire.com

The Taste Cheshire
HOSPITALITY AWARDS

For 15 years, the Taste Cheshire Awards have been honouring the best in the hospitality business across the county.

Last year over 20,000 votes were cast by the public in the Taste Cheshire Awards to herald those that they believe provide that special something for their eating and drinking pleasure, making this one of the most voted for food and drink awards in the UK.

From the start of each year, there is a six-week voting period where people are encouraged to support their favourite establishment in one of 14 categories. Best Large Restaurant has been won three times by Restaurant 1539 and Small Restaurant is always ultra-competitive. Last year the public decided newcomer The Chef's Table was the place to eat. Other awards include Best Pub, which has changed regularly over the years, where at one time a great pint tipped the balance, that now has to be backed up with a strong eating experience. The recent influx of both coffee shops and sandwich bars on the High Street has seen strong opinions formed by the public over what makes these places a "must visit" and it is refreshing to see small independents performing well against the chains every year. The awards also recognise outstanding customer service and best family-friendly venues, however the perennial favourite award has to be Best Sausage!

Recently the CH1ChesterBID Sous Chef Challenge has taken on prominence as MasterChef supremo Gregg Wallace judges the winner at the Chester Food and Drink Festival. This title recognises the amazing contribution that those below the level of Head Chef make in helping to turn out exceptional food night after night.

In an effort to create more individuality for our county's restaurants, the awards also pay tribute to venues who use the most local produce in their menu, and local shops are not overlooked in the awards either.

The job of finding the winners is a difficult one. A venue first has to be voted one of the top four in its category by the public, and after that, each category is mystery dined or shopped by an industry expert who records scores for their visit. It is only after this has been done that the Gold, Silver and Bronze awards can be determined. These awards are amongst the most rigorous and transparent anywhere with each nomination receiving the judges' report after the event. All those nominated truly are winners as they have been recommended by the most important judges in the world – their customers.

An annual dinner held at Chester Racecourse just after Easter each year is the one time of the year that the hospitality trade gets together to let their hair down. Around 400 people attend to hail the winners and those nominated. It's a great night out and a celebration for all the people who truly create "A Taste of Cheshire".

Taste Cheshire

CELERIAC SOUP WITH SMOKED HADDOCK

This is a delicious rich and creamy soup, and the addition of smoked haddock takes it to another level! Serves 4

Ingredients

1 onion, chopped

1 leek, finely chopped

1 garlic bulb, cut through the middle

50g unsalted butter

4 bay leaves

1 celeriac, peeled and diced

2 medium potatoes, peeled and diced

1 litre chicken stock

500ml milk

2 fillets natural smoked haddock

250ml double cream

Method

Sweat the onion, leek and garlic in the butter, together with 2 of the bay leaves. Add the celeriac and potatoes and cook for 10 minutes more, stirring so they don't stick. Pour over enough stock to just about cover then simmer for 20 minutes or until the vegetables are soft.

In a frying pan, bring the milk and the other 2 bay leaves to the boil, then lower to a gentle simmer. Add the fish flesh-side down and poach until just cooked. Remove, flake into a bowl and keep warm.

When the celeriac and potatoes are tender, remove the garlic and bay leaves, add the cream and blitz until smooth.

To serve, put some of the haddock in the bottom of each bowl, and ladle over the soup.

Taste Cheshire
VODKA AND TOMATO RIGATONI

This is a really delicious pasta sauce with a bit of a kick. It's very rich and indulgent and not for those days when you are trying to start your diet.

Serves 4

Ingredients

200g diced pancetta

1 large white onion, finely chopped

1 clove garlic

1-2 dried chillies, finely chopped (or ½ tsp chilli flakes)

125ml vodka

284ml double cream

500ml passata

1 tbsp tomato purée

450g rigatoni pasta

100g freshly grated Parmesan

25g pack of basil, shredded

Freshly ground black pepper

Method

Fry the pancetta in a large frying pan until well browned. Remove from pan and set aside.

In the same pan, fry the onion, garlic and chilli until softened, but not coloured, then add the vodka. Light the vodka and shake the pan gently until flames subside, approximately 2 minutes. Add the cream and boil until sauce thickens.

Add the passata and tomato purée and mix thoroughly.

Add the pancetta back to the pan and simmer gently for a few minutes.

Cook the pasta, drain and put back into the pan. Add the sauce, the Parmesan cheese, fresh basil and freshly ground black pepper, mix well and serve.

BRAISED PORK CHEEKS WITH BLACK BEANS

A cheap cut transformed by long, slow cooking to make a tender succulent stew
that needs nothing more than some buttered spinach or a crisp green salad.

Serves 4

Ingredients

2 tbsp plain flour

12 pork cheeks, trimmed

2 tbsp oil

200g smoked bacon lardons

50g unsalted butter

3 banana shallots, finely sliced

30g runny honey

1 tbsp fresh thyme leaves

200ml dry cider

200ml chicken stock

1 tbsp wholegrain mustard

100ml double cream

400g tin black beans, well rinsed

1 tbsp balsamic vinegar

2 tbsp chopped parsley

Salt and freshly ground black pepper

Method

You will need a large, shallow ovenproof casserole dish with a lid. Preheat the oven to 160°C/140°C Fan/Gas 3.

Combine the flour with some salt and pepper in a shallow dish, then dust the pork cheeks all over with the seasoned flour.

Heat the oil in the casserole dish over a medium heat and fry the pork cheeks for 2-3 minutes, or until browned on all sides. Remove the pork and set aside.

Fry the lardons until crisp and brown, then remove from the dish and set aside.

In the same dish, melt the butter, then add the shallots and fry gently for 5 minutes. Add the honey and stir to coat. Return the cheeks and lardons to the casserole and add the thyme, cider and chicken stock. Place in the preheated oven, covered with a lid and cook for 2½ hours.

Remove the pork cheeks from the casserole and set aside to rest. Add the mustard, cream, black beans and vinegar, cooking for a further 5-6 minutes. Return the cheeks to the dish to coat in the sauce, sprinkle with parsley and serve.

Taste Cheshire
CHOCOLATE MOUSSE

A really easy chocolatey mousse that works every time. For extra indulgence, top with a dollop of double cream and some fresh berries. Serves 4

Ingredients

150g good-quality dark chocolate

4 large eggs

50g caster sugar

150ml double cream

1 tbsp good-quality cocoa powder

Method

Place the chocolate in a heatproof bowl over a pan of gently simmering water and leave to melt.

Separate the eggs – whites in one bowl, yolks in the other. Add the sugar to the bowl of yolks and beat until it has dissolved and the mixture is silky and smooth.

Whisk the whites until they form soft peaks.

In a third bowl, beat the cream until slightly thick and just whipped.

Once the chocolate has melted, carefully lift the bowl out of the pan.

Add the cocoa powder to your bowl of yolks and mix well.

Tip in the cream and mix again, then fold through the melted chocolate until it's well combined and a gorgeous colour.

Finish by tipping in the egg whites, then keep folding, from the outside in in a figure-of-eight until the mix is smooth and evenly coloured. Spoon or ladle into your chosen serving dish or glasses and put in the fridge for a couple of hours to set.

Blooming DELICIOUS

First-class shopping for the home and garden is complemented by a range of exquisite dining destinations at Bents Garden & Home, where a passion for exceptional service, beautiful presentation and fine ingredients has set the culinary bar high.

The Bents story begins back in the 1930s with the famous roses grown by Alfred and Margaret Bent. Their beautifully adorned terrace house was the talk of the village, and after selling their roses locally, the green-fingered couple eventually bought their first plot of land in the 1950s.

As the family expanded and grew, so did the business. Today three generations of the Bent family have been involved in creating the stunning garden centre with its impressive dining destinations. What hasn't changed, and has always remained at the heart of the business, is the friendly welcome and warm atmosphere.

Alongside the stunning home and garden shopping facilities, Bents is now equally famous for its dining options. Just as the family have always grown their plants themselves, they insist on all the food being freshly prepared on the premises, too.

The Fresh Approach Restaurant is the heart and soul of the Bents experience, and its name says everything you need to know about its offerings – think breakfast cooked to order, freshly baked jacket potatoes, homemade soups, salads you can create yourself and a range of hand-crafted pâtisseries. The traditional counter-style service and light and airy atmosphere make it the perfect spot for lunch.

And, just like the luxury shopping options, there is a dining destination for every occasion – from Caffè Lago by the outdoor play area, ideal for sunny afternoons, to the brand new Caffè nel Verde and The Fresh Express. There is even a fabulous area for you to enjoy food with your four-legged friends – indulge your pets with a treat at The Pet Cafe while you enjoy a speciality coffee and cake.

The latest addition sees an exciting new Tapas Bar, which brings a taste of the Mediterranean to the Centre – enjoy a selection of authentic Spanish bites and explore the wonderful selection of wines.

Whichever destination you choose, the freshest locally-sourced ingredients ensure that every homemade dish will be a palate-pleaser. The team of 18 chefs make everything in-house to the finest standards and the presentation is just as beautiful as the home and garden displays.

The family-run business has a reputation for quality, experience and innovation when it comes to its understanding of exclusive living. From the culinary options on offer, it's clear that this passion extends to achieving the very best quality in catering, too.

Bents Garden & Home
SPICY PORK MEATBALLS

This spicy Spanish-inspired dish is a favourite at our Tapas Bar and with this quick and easy recipe you can re-create it at home. All of the ingredients are available from our Food Hall and Honeywell's Butchers. Serve with a tomato and basil sauce. Serves 4

Ingredients

300g fresh pork mince from Honeywell's Butchers

150g nduja paste

25g parsley, finely chopped

A pinch of salt

25ml cooking oil

Tomato and basil sauce and crusty white bread, to serve

Method

Preheat the oven to 180°C.

In a mixing bowl, combine the pork mince with the nduja paste. (The 'nduja paste will need breaking up and rubbing between your fingers to help soften into the pork evenly). Add the finely chopped parsley and salt then mix well.

Roll one 20g ball from the mixture and fry this to check the seasoning. Once happy, roll the rest of the mixture into 20g balls. Roast in the preheated oven with the oil for 10-12 minutes or until fully cooked through – the meatballs should not be pink in the middle.

Serve with a tomato and basil sauce with slices of crusty bread.

Bents Garden & Home

MUSHROOM SOUP

This is a great, hearty, warming soup that can be as extravagant as you want!
The dish works well with most mushrooms – fresh porcini, shiitake, chestnut
and button being the popular choices. Serves 2

Ingredients

300g fresh mushrooms

Butter, for frying

1 medium white onion

1 medium potato

1 dessertspoon cooking oil

1 garlic clove

500ml vegetable or mushroom stock

A few sprigs of fresh thyme

1 dessertspoon mascarpone

1 dessertspoon butter

Truffle oil

Salt & pepper

Method

Clean and break the mushrooms into quarters, and brown them in a frying pan with butter and set aside.

Meanwhile, peel and chop the onion, crush the garlic and sweat until softened in a little oil, add most of the mushrooms but keep a few back for later. Peel and chop the potato into 1cm cubes and add to the onion and mushroom mix. Top with the stock and add the thyme, allow to simmer gently for approximately 10 minutes or until the potato and mushrooms are tender.

Once tender, remove the thyme and then blend until smooth with a spoon of mascarpone, and a touch of seasoning. Scatter the remaining mushrooms over the top as you serve.

For that extra special garnish, add a drizzle of truffle oil.

A Roaring
SUCCESS

Sizzling BBQs and meats slow-roasted to perfection –
Big 5 Catering can't guarantee the African sunshine at your event,
but they can certainly deliver the warm atmosphere and fantastic flavours
that come with their South African-inspired catering.

When Darren Andrews moved to the UK from South Africa in 2001, he brought with him the memories of warm summer evenings spent standing around the BBQ surrounded by friends and family, not to mention those fantastic flavours. Inspired by his home country, he launched his South African-inspired catering service – the Big 5 is an old hunting term for the most dangerous animals to hunt (lion, leopard, elephant, rhino and buffalo), but today these incredible animals are the ones people want to see on a safari trip.

The simplicity of roasting meat and the irresistible aromas, tastes and textures this age-old cooking method creates never fail to delight crowds. It forms the ultimate food theatre, making it perfect for celebratory gatherings and special events.

Known as a 'braai', the South African BBQ will stand out in everybody's memories. Alongside burgers, steaks and sticky pork ribs, guests can choose to try famous boerewors (South African sausages), sosaties (kebabs in a secret marinade) or springbok, zebra, crocodile or buffalo for the more adventurous. Big 5 Catering are also famous for their hog roasts and lamb spits.

For Darren, along with his incredible marinades, the quality of the meat is what makes his BBQs, hog roasts and lamb spits truly special. He sources all his meat from a local award-winning butcher to ensure the very finest results. He does all the cooking on-site where possible – whether it's a braai or a hog roast that needs over 8 hours – for the ultimate freshness and tender results. Darren is a BBQ specialist and can cook every piece of meat to perfection.

If you would prefer classic British flavours, you can opt for a hog roast with roast apple purée and homemade stuffing, or a lamb spit with minty yoghurt or homemade aioli. Whatever your preference, the team at Big 5 Catering are happy to work out a menu to suit you. Along with a selection of salads (the biltong and potato salad is always a winner!) Darren's wife Alayne creates glorious desserts to suit the occasion. Her malva pudding is popular, as is the indulgent milk tart.

From street parties, markets and corporate events to weddings, christenings and birthdays, for Darren being part of someone's special occasion is the best part of his job. "It's a privilege to be part of any event and every member of the Big 5 team works over and above to make sure everyone has a truly memorable day."

NoWFOO
The N Big 5 Catering

BIG 5
SAUCES
South African Style

BIG 5
SAUCES
South African Style
ZINGY
BBQ
250g

BIG 5
SAUCES
South African Style!
CAPE
MALAY
CURRY
SAUCE
375g

BIG 5
CATERING
BBQ & Hog Roast South Afri
big5catering.co.uk   07834

Big 5 Catering
CAPE MALAY MILD CHICKEN CURRY BUNNY CHOW

The recipe below has been slightly altered compared to the Cape Malay Cooking Sauce, which we retail, making it perfect for trying at home. Bunny Chow is a South African dish of curry served in a hollowed-out bread loaf. Serves 4

Ingredients

4 tbsp rapeseed oil

2 medium onions, roughly chopped into medium-sized chunks

1 large red pepper, seeded and roughly chopped into medium-sized chunks

1 large garlic clove, finely chopped

1 tbsp garam masala*

½ tsp ground turmeric*

½ tsp cinnamon powder*

½ tsp ground cardamom*

¼ tsp curry leaf powder (or two curry leaves)*

1 tin of chopped tomatoes (400g)

100g dried apricots, halved

125ml hot water

½ tsp salt

500g chicken breast, diced into medium-sized chunks

1 loaf of bread (brown or white), cut in four, and soft middle removed to make four bread bowls (Reserve the soft bread for dipping. An optional extra is to line the inside of each "bread bowl" with butter.)

* I like to mix the spices in a small bowl so when they are added to the cooking process they can be constantly stirred so they don't burn.

Method

Add 2 tbsp of the oil to a pan and heat over a medium heat. Add the onions, red pepper and garlic and cook to soften. Add the spices and stir for about 30 seconds, making sure they don't burn (they might stick to the base of the pan, but keep stirring and get the flavours into the onion and pepper – once you add the water and tomatoes it will deglaze the pan).

Add the chopped tomatoes, apricots, water and salt and let it simmer on a low heat with the pan lid on – don't let the sauce dry out or reduce down too much.

While the sauce is simmering, add two tablespoons of oil to a frying pan and set over a medium heat. Cook the diced chicken until it is cooked through and browned on the outside.

Once the chicken is cooked through, add the Cape Malay sauce to the same pan and stir to give the chicken a nice coating. (Note: the Cape Malay sauce should be quite wet and not too thick, so it soaks nicely into the bread.)

Add the curry to your bread bowl and using the soft bit of bread you scooped out, dip it into the curry. Eat the rest how you please, but this dish is certain to be a talking point at any dinner party or social gathering.

Variations

If you want to spice it up a bit more, you can add a ¼ teaspoon of chilli powder to your spice mix or 2 freshly chopped red chillies to the onion, garlic and pepper.

An optional extra is to add Greek yoghurt, diced fresh tomato and red onion to finish off your Bunny!

This recipe also works well with lamb and pork. Why not use leftovers from your pork, lamb or chicken roast, reheat and add the sauce.

This sauce can easily be made in advance and kept in the fridge or freezer and added to your favourite meat at a later stage – like most cooking sauces it does get better after a day or so in the fridge.

It is also worth noting that Bunny Chow is not restricted to curry, you can do it with chilli con carne; bacon (diced), sausage (diced), beans and egg, or anything else. The options are endless!

A Bitter 'Bout BREWING

The father and son team behind The Brew Foundation, one of Cheshire's most exciting independent breweries, admit to being just a little bit obsessed when it comes to beer...

For James Eardley and his dad Robert, the first brew came about in the same way many people decide to have a go at brewing their own beer... over a conversation in the local watering hole. However, the Eardley family don't do things by halves – they decided they wanted to create "the most drinkable beers on the planet."

After many years of research, what started out as an idea suddenly became a reality when they were offered the chance to brew out of one of Cheshire's famous breweries, Wincle Beer Company. Known as "cuckoo brewing", it gave them the opportunity to benefit from Wincle's experience of craft brewing, while having the freedom to pursue their own brewing adventure.

The aim of The Brew Foundation was quite simple – to make beers they liked to drink themselves. "I call them session beers," says James. "We didn't want to make the strongest beers in the world; we wanted them to be the most enjoyable. If someone orders a second pint of one of our beers, we've achieved success!"

The first beer they developed, First Light, is an American pale ale, which is clean and crisp with a delicate hoppy citrus flavour. Second came Bitter That, which is a fruity, malty bitter that is light enough for summer drinking and comforting enough for winter. It has proved a real success in many Cheshire pubs, rattling a few bartenders with its playful name... "I'll have a Bitter That please."... "A bit of what?"... You get the picture! The third offering came in the form of an utterly drinkable session IPA, Hops & Dreams. At 4%, they describe this one as, "easy-drinking enough to be a great session ale, but at the same time packed with enough hop character to satisfy any hop head."

The fourth (Hop & Glory) is currently being perfected, but it is planned to be the bigger brother of Hops & Dreams, encompassing the same hops but stronger and packed with flavour. There is also talk of an exciting collaboration with their friends at Wincle. The rumour is that it will be a porter... but we'll just have to wait patiently to find out!

James now lives in Sheffield and handles sales at that side of the Pennines, while Robert is based in Cheshire, so between them, they are making sure The Brew Foundation is becoming a familiar brand across the North. Look out for their beers at pubs and bottle shops throughout Cheshire, Sheffield, Stoke on Trent, Manchester and Wakefield.

The Brew Foundation
STEAK, KIDNEY & A BITTER THAT PIE

My mum Lynda uses Bitter That in her classic steak and kidney pie recipe and it's always a winner in our family. You will need a lidded casserole dish that can go on the hob and into the oven and a pie dish. Serves 6

Ingredients

4 tbsp oil

2 onions, chopped

25g flour

1kg stewing beef, diced into 2cm pieces

3 lamb's kidneys, middle white bits removed, chopped

400ml Bitter That

300ml beef stock

25g butter

500g mushrooms, sliced

Pack of ready-made puff pastry

1 egg, lightly beaten

Sea salt and pepper

Method

Preheat the oven to 160°C/140°C fan/Gas 3.

Heat 1 tbsp of the oil in an ovenproof casserole and gently fry the onions for about 5 minutes until soft. Remove with a slotted spoon and set aside.

Season the flour and toss the steak and kidney in it. Add a little more oil to the pan and, over a medium heat, brown the meat. You may have to do this in batches. Remove with a slotted spoon and set aside.

Add some of the beer to the pan to deglaze it. Scrape well using a wooden spatula and then add the rest of the beer and the stock. Return the onions, steak and kidney to the casserole and gradually bring to the boil, stirring well.

Put a lid on the casserole and place in the oven for 1 hour 30 minutes.

Heat the butter in a frying pan. Add the mushrooms and fry briskly for a couple of minutes. Stir into the casserole. Continue to cook for a further hour.

Remove from the oven, check the seasoning and leave to cool.

Allow the pastry to come up to room temperature and then follow the instructions on the pack. Turn up the oven to 220°C/200°C fan/Gas 7.

Spoon the pie filling into a suitable pie dish. Place the pastry over the filling, trim and crimp the edges. Make a hole in the middle for the steam to escape. Brush the surface of the pie with the beaten egg. Bake for about 30 minutes until the pastry is golden brown.

Cheshire's FARM SHOP

A well-stocked farm shop, butchery, bakery, delicatessen and vibrant café, the array of local produce on offer at Cheerbrook is as impressive as their string of accolades.

Andrew and Sarah Shufflebotham opened Cheerbrook in October 2000. With farming backgrounds and a love of local produce, they began their business at farmers' markets. Receiving positive feedback from customers and with lots of people saying they'd like to be able to visit them more regularly, they decided to open a small farm shop. Their aim was simply to provide top-quality food to the local community, offering good value for money and excellent customer service.

Over the years, Cheerbrook has evolved into one of Cheshire's finest farm shops. The butchery was always at the centre of the business and in 2014 it was crowned 'Best On-Farm Butchery' at the FARMA awards. Whole carcasses are butchered on-site so they can offer all the traditional cuts as well as some lesser known pieces of meat. Their handmade sausages are made with free-range local pork – and it's fair to say the Cheerbrook butchers are bonkers about their bangers. They have travelled the length and breadth of the country researching other sausages! All that taste-testing paid off – nearly every one of their sausages has an award to its name.

A bakery and delicatessen are also popular with Cheshire residents. From Mark's famous pork pies (also award-winners!) to Debbie's fabulous cakes and puddings, everything is cooked fresh on the premises daily. The kitchen is also a hive of activity. Cheerbrook chefs whip up scrummy meals, just as you would at home (nothing artificial added) and portion them out into fresh ready meals that make the most of the meat from the butchers counter and the best-quality ingredients from the farm shop. Lasagne, cottage pie, lamb in red wine, fish pie… perfect for when you want the finest home-cooked meal but don't have the time to spend hours in the kitchen.

Although today Cheerbrook has grown into a premier farm shop, what has always been important to Andrew and Sarah is that it is still somewhere people can get their everyday essentials. For regulars, this is a place to stop by a few times a week to pick up all their basics at honest prices – bread, milk, eggs, fresh vegetables, fruits, store-cupboard essentials. Everything is sourced from trusted local suppliers who are committed to the same values as the Cheerbrook team, so why not pop in and try the vast array of amazing produce grown or made here in Cheshire?

Cheerbrook
COTTAGE PIE WITH
BUBBLE & SQUEAK TOPPING

Made with lean Cheerbrook mince, this cottage pie with a twist from our Ready Meal range is always a best-seller. Easy to make (even easier when you buy it ready made from us), comforting and nutritious, just serve with steamed broccoli or kale for a meal that will tick all the boxes. Serves 4-6

Ingredients

1 tbsp vegetable oil

1 onion, peeled and finely chopped

2 carrots, peeled and finely chopped

450g Cheerbrook lean minced beef

1 tbsp plain flour

1 tbsp tomato purée

1 tbsp Worcestershire sauce

300ml hot beef stock

900g potatoes, peeled and chopped

170g Savoy cabbage, thinly sliced

3 spring onions, thinly sliced

Knob of butter

Milk

Salt and freshly milled black pepper

Method

Preheat the oven to 190°C/Gas 5.

Heat the oil in a pan, add the onion and carrots and cook to soften. Add the mince and fry until browned. Stir in the flour, tomato purée and Worcestershire sauce and cook for a minute. Add the hot stock, little by little, and bring to the boil, then simmer for 5 minutes.

Meanwhile, in a large pan, place the potatoes in salted water and bring to the boil. Cook for 20 minutes or until soft. During the last 10 minutes of cooking time, add the cabbage.

Lightly fry the spring onions to soften them. Mash the potatoes and cabbage with the butter and milk, and combine with the spring onions. Season to taste.

Transfer the mince into an ovenproof dish and spoon the bubble and squeak mash over the top. Cook in the preheated oven for 25-30 minutes until golden brown.

Cheerbrook
TEA LOAF

The Cheerbrook tea loaf is one of our most popular cakes, delicious and moist enough to eat by itself or if you're feeling naughty smother with creamy farmhouse butter. All you need to do then is curl up with a cup of tea in a comfy chair and relax, well until you can't resist another slice that is! Serves 8

Ingredients

175g currants

175g sultanas

225g light muscovado sugar

300ml strong hot tea

1 large free-range egg

275g self-raising flour

Method

Put the fruit and sugar into a bowl and pour over the hot tea, cover and leave overnight.

Preheat the oven to 150°C/Fan 130°C/Gas 2. Lightly grease a 900g loaf tin and line the base with baking parchment.

Lightly beat the egg, then stir this and the flour into the fruit mixture, mix thoroughly then pour into the prepared tin and level the surface.

Bake in the preheated oven for about 90 minutes or until well risen and firm to the touch. A skewer inserted into the centre should come out clean. Leave to cool in the tin for 10 minutes then turn out, peel off the parchment and finish cooling on a wire rack.

Serve sliced and buttered.

Bringing something new to
THE TABLE

With a waiting list for weekend bookings, a listing in the 2016 Michelin guide and two AA rosettes already under its belt, this tiny restaurant in the centre of Chester has got everybody talking – take a seat at The Chef's Table...

For the small team behind The Chef's Table, it's unbelievable to think their unique eatery only opened its doors in April 2014. Opened on a shoestring budget and tucked away down a side street, the miniscule premises have no storeroom, no walk-in fridge, no wine cellar – it isn't just a cosy restaurant, it's decidedly tiny.

The owners have been in many different areas of the industry all their lives, working in some of the region's best establishments and constantly striving to learn more, to cook better, to push boundaries. For chef-owner Liam McKay, he wanted to put his fine-dining expertise and his inexhaustible creativity in an environment that was more relaxed and enjoyable.

To follow their dream and open The Chef's Table in one of Chester's hidden corners took a leap of faith and a huge amount of dedication. The tiny kitchen forms the heart of the restaurant. Completely open to view, it forms the stage for theatre like no other. The level of cooking that goes on in the small space is fascinating. They began with just two chefs, but today six talented chefs work alongside Liam McKay to create unique and extraordinary plates.

The menu is never the same two weeks in a row. Partly because Liam never runs out of inspiration or the drive to try new things, and partly thanks to their exclusive relationship with The Natural Veg Men. These neighbouring food-lovers are the team's good friends and allies in the pursuit of pushing boundaries when it comes to seasonal cooking. They passionately grow their fruit and vegetables within 15 miles of the restaurant. They nurture a unique and intrinsic relationship with The Chef's Table in that they have the freedom to grow some really unusual produce and then Liam has the opportunity to experiment with it in his menus – the electric daisy was one of 2015's most exciting ingredients to take centre stage on one of his dishes.

Creativity doesn't end with the food, though. The homemade soft drinks are really worth a try and the cocktails and wine list offer true originality that show they are much more than afterthoughts. With regularly changing artwork adorning the walls and eclectic music in the background, the atmosphere can change alongside the menus.

Just a year after opening, Open Table ranked The Chef's Table third in their Top 100 restaurants in the UK – an incredible achievement for the team. With a mention in the 2016 Michelin guide and a huge string of accolades already accrued, it's no wonder there is a waiting list for this gastronomic gem.

The Chefs Table
PRAWNS IN TWO PARTS

Head Chef Liam has created this beautiful prawn dish that is sure to impress any guests! Serves 1

Ingredients

4 tiger prawns, deshelled and deveined (reserve shells)

1 leaf Castle Franco radicchio

1 leaf red chicory

½ cucumber, peeled and sliced on a mandoline

½ avocado, sliced

100g brown shrimps

2 sprigs monk's beard agretti

Lemon dressing:

Juice of 2 lemons

1 tsp caster sugar

1 tsp Dijon mustard

200ml olive oil

Avocado emulsion :

½ avocado

1 tbsp lemon juice

1 tbsp mayonnaise

Saffron emulsion:

3g saffron

10ml hot water

1 tbsp mayonnaise

Squid ink emulsion:

10g squid ink

1 tbsp mayonnaise

1 tbsp lemon juice

Red pepper/prawn/tomato emulsion:

4 prawn shells

100ml white wine

½ red pepper, sliced

10 cherry tomatoes, halved

1 tsp xanthan gum

1 tsp caster sugar

1 tsp paprika

1 tbsp white wine vinegar

1 tbsp mayonnaise

Marie rose:

1 tbsp pepper emulsion

1 tbsp tomato ketchup

1 tsp brandy

1 tsp Worcester sauce

1 tsp lemon juice

Method

Make the lemon dressing by reducing the lemon juice, sugar and Dijon to a syrup in a pan, then chill. Whisk in the oil slowly, season and leave to one side.

Now make the emulsions. For the avocado emulsion, blend with the lemon juice and mayonnaise, season and pass through a fine chinois or sieve. Place in a squirty bottle.

For the saffron emulsion, steep the saffron in the hot water until the water starts turning yellow, then blend with the mayonnaise and pass through a fine chinois or sieve. Place in a squirty bottle.

For the squid ink emulsion, blend the squid ink with the lemon juice and mayonnaise, and pass through a fine chinois or sieve. Place in a squirty bottle.

For the red pepper emulsion, preheat the oven to 180°C. Roast the prawn shells on a roasting tray in the preheated oven for 12 minutes. Add the wine to the tray to deglaze and pass through a fine chinois or sieve, reserving the liquid and discarding the shells. Now add the wine to all the other ingredients (apart from the mayonnaise) in a saucepan and cook on a stove top until the tomatoes have broken down and the peppers are really soft. Blend, season and pass through a fine chinois or sieve, then chill. Once chilled, reserve 1 tbsp of the red pepper emulsion for the Marie Rose and blend the rest with the mayonnaise. Place in a squirty bottle.

For the Marie Rose whisk all ingredients together, season and place in squirty bottle.

To assemble, you will need one glass, one plate, four skewers and a food-safe paint tube.

Skewer the prawns so they stay straight when cooking and season them. Grill the prawns for around 3-4 minutes, until cooked. While the prawns are cooking, dress the salad leaves, cucumber, avocado and brown shrimps with the lemon dressing, and start building your salad in the glass. Finish with a good dollop of Marie Rose.

Now move on to your plate. Fill your tube with avocado emulsion, seal, then squeeze out onto the plate. Dot the other emulsions to resemble paint on the plate. Dress the monk's beard with lemon dressing, then place on the plate. Finally place two cooked prawns on the salad and two on the plate. Serve, sit back and listen to everyone moaning that it's pretentious and you should keep things simple! Bon appetite, Liam.

The View from
THE FIELDS

Just four miles from Chester city centre, The Chester Fields is a country pub and popular restaurant with stunning views over the Cheshire countryside.

The two Directors of The Chester Fields have been friends since school, and they have injected their interests and personalities into their popular dining pub, which opened its doors in 2011. Everything in the design has something personal to the pair, such as the outdoor heated mountain ski huts and bar, which are reminders of their personal affiliation to Austria.

The location of the pub in the beautiful Cheshire countryside has led to the outdoor areas becoming a focus for its customers – in fact it has 100 seats outside in addition to its 120 indoor covers. This is thanks to the stunning views it commands over the Cheshire plains – it's a beer garden and outdoor dining area like no other, making it incredibly popular during the summer months.

Whether you are dining inside the cosy country pub interior or in the show-stopping outdoor garden, the menu contains a selection of mouthwatering delights made with locally-sourced ingredients. They've won several awards, such as Best in Local Produce and Best Large Restaurant at the Taste Cheshire Food and Drink Awards, and their dedication to using fine local produce has earned them a solid reputation as one of Cheshire's best dining venues.

The Head Chef Ian Worley, who has previously worked for Alex Polizzi (The Hotel Inspector) and also at The Midland Hotel in Manchester, uses skill and creativity to create dishes to suit the ambience, from British classics and light lunches to impressive evening meals. Working alongside the MD, Mark Jarvis, who trained for five years at The Savoy Hotel in London, it's safe to say there is a lot of experience within The Chester Fields team! The excellent food and service go hand-in-hand with the relaxed and welcoming atmosphere – it is testament to the lively and dynamic team spirit that is evident from the kitchens to the front of house staff and bar.

They love to break the rules of the hospitality industry at The Chester Fields and have become known for their unique offers and events that are distinctly outside the box – from hosting events with extravagant prizes (from a stay in a penthouse apartment in the Austrian mountains with all flights and transfers to a £1000 holiday voucher!) to raising thousands of pounds for charities such as MNDA, The Christie Charity and Emily Ffion Trust.

Due to the incredible setting and commitment to service, weddings are very popular at The Chester Fields, as well as other private events. With plans for expansion in the pipeline, the team look forward to being able to welcome even more people to enjoy this premier venue with its unbeatable views.

The Chester Fields
LAMB SHOULDER HOT POT

There are a few elements to this dish, but the pickled red cabbage can be made a day in advance. It is a lovely impressive dish for serving to guests. Serves 4-6

Ingredients

Shoulder of lamb:

6 cloves garlic, finely chopped

2 large sprigs of rosemary, finely chopped

1 lamb shoulder (approx. 2kg), boned, rolled and tied (ask your butcher to do this)

500ml chicken stock

Salt and pepper

Olive oil, for coating

Pomme-Anna:

400g butter

6 cloves garlic, thinly sliced

2 sprigs of rosemary, leaves picked

8 large Maris Piper potatoes

Salt and pepper

Pickled red cabbage:

1 red cabbage, quartered, cored and finely shredded

120ml malt vinegar

120ml Balsamic vinegar

120ml white wine vinegar

330g white sugar

2 cinnamon sticks, snapped in half

1 tsp black peppercorns

1 tsp dried chillies

6 bay leaves

2 star anise

2 tsp coriander seeds

2 tsp salt

Ale-braised onions:

2 large white onions, peeled and sliced into very thin rings

½ pint ale

100g butter

20g caster sugar

Method

Shoulder of lamb

Rub the chopped garlic and rosemary into the lamb shoulder. Leave to marinate in the fridge for 4 hours.

Preheat the oven to 140°C. Scrape off the rosemary and garlic and keep to one side. Preheat a griddle pan or BBQ. Season the lamb with salt and pepper and rub with olive oil. Place in the hot pan and sear to put nice golden brown bar marks evenly over the lamb shoulder. Place in an ovenproof dish and pour the chicken stock over adding the reserved garlic and rosemary. Cover the dish with tin foil or a lid and place in the oven to cook for 3 – 4 hours, until tender. Cook for longer if needed.

Pomme-Anna

Preheat the oven to 160°C. Melt the butter with the garlic and rosemary. Peel the potatoes then slice them as thinly as possible. Layer the potatoes in an ovenproof dish, seasoning every layer with salt and pepper as you go. Strain the rosemary and garlic from the butter and pour evenly over the potatoes. Cover with tin foil and roast in the oven for approximately 1½ hours until cooked golden brown.

Pickled red cabbage

Salt the cabbage and leave in a colander for 2-3 hours until a deeper red colour. Whilst the cabbage is draining, make the pickling liquor. Put all the other ingredients together in a pan and cover tightly with cling film. Gently bring to the boil and remove instantly. Leave to cool and infuse.

Rinse off the cabbage, pat dry and put into a bowl. Bring the pickle liquor back to the boil then strain through a fine sieve onto the cabbage. Cover with cling film and leave to cool. When cooled, transfer to an airtight container.

Ale-braised onions

Preheat the oven to 160°C. Put the onion slices into an ovenproof dish with the ale, butter and sugar then cover with parchment paper. Roast in the oven for 1½-2 hours until the onions have caramelized and gone sticky. Stir occasionally while roasting.

To serve

Make the red cabbage a day in advance. Start the lamb shoulder and place in the oven. When the lamb is in the oven, start the ale-braised onions. Start the pomme-Anna. When the lamb is cooked, remove it from the stock and allow it to rest on a rack or plate. Strain the cooking liquor then reduce in a pan, skimming off the fat until the flavour is intensified and you have a sauce-like consistency. Remove the string from the lamb and carve a large piece for each person. Pour over the sauce, top with the onions then serve with the pomme-Anna and room-temperature red cabbage. Garnish with a nice bunch of watercress dressed with a little vinaigrette.

Chester
TOWN CRIERS

Oyez … Oyez … Oyez!

David and Julie Mitchell are the country's first husband and wife town crier partnership. The town criers have long been a treasured connection to Chester's historic past – historically they would have announced the news to the town's people. Today they are unique as they still have regular noon proclamations from the High Cross five days a week during the summer.

There is a lovely story behind David and Julie's unusual occupation… David had booked a town crier to wake Julie on the morning of their wedding 26 years ago. Unfortunately, the town crier was unable to attend at the last minute. David, not one to give up easily, decided that he would perform the role himself! It was a successful day with David enjoying the experience so much that when the role was advertised he jumped at the chance to take it on! Julie joined him a few years later and the pair have never looked back.

David and Julie act as costumed after dinner speakers, travelling all over the country. They have worked with hundreds of clients in every context – royal, civic, council, corporate, association, entertainment, film, TV, radio and print. They look forward to working with plenty more people in the future, helping clients with all their attention-grabbing and people-organising needs.

The Coach House is their favourite place to eat, as they love its historic setting in the centre of Chester and its heritage as a coach house. Won over by the charm of the atmosphere, the friendly staff and the delicious locally-sourced food, they are regulars in this lovely pub.

The Coach House
FISHCAKES

This is one of David and Julie's favourite dishes from The Coach House.
Makes 10-15

Ingredients

6 large potatoes

4 cod fillets, about 225g each, skinned and pin-boned

2 cups milk

1 lemon, roughly sliced

2 bay leaves

1 bag of spinach

200g cheddar cheese, grated

6 eggs, hard-boiled and peeled

4 egg yolks

100g plain flour

300g breadcrumbs

Method

Preheat the oven to 160°C. Peel the potatoes and boil in salted water until soft, then mash. Poach the cod in the milk with the lemon and bay leaves, and drain when cooked. Add the spinach and cheddar and chop through, then add the potato and mix everything together. Grate the hard-boiled eggs into the mixture and stir in. Form the mixture into small patties.

Place the egg yolks in one bowl, the flour in a second bowl and the breadcrumbs in a third bowl. Place the patties first into the flour, then into the egg yolk and finally into the bread crumbs. Place on a baking tray and cook in the preheated oven to cook for 35 minutes.

Cheshire's STAR

The jewel in Cheshire's culinary crown, Simon Radley at The Chester Grosvenor has retained its Michelin star since 1990 and is revered as one of the UK's finest restaurants.

The Chester Grosvenor is a stunning building. It stands proudly in the heart of this historic city amongst the cobbled streets and preserved architecture. The elegant charm of the hotel is the perfect setting for Simon Radley's stunning restaurant.

The string of accolades is far too long to list in full, but with four AA rosettes and a Michelin star, it is clear that this restaurant is a cut above its rivals. In fact it was voted as Best Hotel Restaurant at the European Hospitality Awards in 2015, as well as being listed in the top 100 restaurants in the UK by the Sunday Times. Retaining a Michelin star for over 25 years is testament to the unfailing commitment to excellence and attention to detail that makes each dining experience special.

A top-quality meal made using the finest seasonal ingredients must be accompanied by the perfect glass of wine. The resident sommelier at Simon Radley at The Chester Grosvenor is always on hand to assist diners with advice and recommendations. Since the wine cellar is one of the most extensive in England (with over 1000 bins from around the world), the sommelier's friendly advice is usually very much appreciated.

From the welcoming charm of the front of house staff and the subtly attentive service to the atmosphere of chic sophistication, the stage for Simon Radley's culinary creativity is set from the moment you enter the restaurant. Whether you opt for the tasting menu or the à la carte, prepare to be wowed by the beauty and flavours of every mouthful.

Simon Radley at The Chester Grosvenor

Simon Radley at The Chester Grosvenor
DEXTER BEEF RIB, PARSLEY-BUTTERED CARROTS AND ONION TARTE TATIN

A beautiful dish using the finest Dexter beef and locally-sourced Cheshire vegetables. Serves 2

Ingredients

8 baby carrots

125g salted butter, softened to room temperature

30g picked flat leaf or curly parsley, roughly chopped

1 small white-skinned onion

Puff pastry

2 egg yolks

200g caster sugar

1 tbsp red wine vinegar

Double beef rib chop

Salt and black pepper

Oil, for cooking

Picked watercress tips, to garnish

Method

For the carrots, trim the green top off then peel from top to bottom. Gently scrape where the carrot meets the green top, removing any dirt. In salted simmering water, cook the carrots for 4 minutes – test with the tip of a knife to ensure they are cooked. Refresh immediately in ice water. Drain on a J-cloth and set aside in the fridge.

For the parsley butter, add the butter and chopped parsley to a food processor and mix until incorporated. Lay out some cling film and roll the butter mix into sausages. Tie the ends of the cling film and place in the fridge to harden.

For the onion tatins, preheat the oven to 180°C. Cut the onion in half across the middle. Warm a little oil in a pan and cook the onion until it is caramelised and golden brown. Remove from the pan and allow to cool.

Peel the skin from the onion and place on a board cooked-side down. Cut two discs of puff pastry using a 7.5cm pastry cutter and mould over the onion, making sure the pastry completely covers the onion. With a fork, gently prick the pastry. Using a pastry brush, coat the pastry with the egg yolk. Place in the fridge until needed.

Heat a heavy-bottomed saucepan and add half of the sugar. Heat until melted then add the remaining sugar and cook until golden brown. Carefully add the vinegar and stir until incorporated. Pour the caramel into two foil pastry cases, making sure the bottom is covered. Place the onion tatin in the caramel and gently press down. Cook in the preheated oven for 13 minutes.

To finish, cook the double beef rib chop to your liking, allow to rest, then carve into slices and present back onto the bone. Reheat the carrots in boiling salted water and season with salt and pepper. Place the carrots in a warm pan with the parsley butter. Serve the carrots on top of the beef. Gently remove the tatins from the caramel and serve on the side, then garnish with picked watercress tips.

Once upon a CHIME

The awards are quickly stacking up for this new Hartford wine bar – versatile menus and a unique drinks selection, there is something for everyone at Chime.

Set in an intriguing building in the centre of Hartford, Chime is a thoroughly modern wine bar that has embraced its historic past – we'll come on to that curious name shortly... For Sarah and Liz, the ambitious owners, who have another highly successful financial recruitment business, along with Scott (General Manager) and Elliott (Head Chef), it has been the project of a lifetime and the product of a shared love of food, wine and hospitality.

Sarah and Liz are known by all around them as warm, friendly and honest – and their wine bar embodies all of these traits in bucket-loads. The welcoming atmosphere has embedded it firmly in the heart of its community and already won it recognition for Excellence in Customer Service at the 2015 Taste Cheshire Awards, alongside the coveted Best Newcomer Award.

Manager Scott and Head Chef Elliott met 6 years ago and, since then, have always worked together. So when the pair met Liz and Sarah and talked about their wine bar idea, they realised this was the dream opportunity to bring something new and exciting to the area and create something truly special.

The menus are diverse so there is something for everyone on any day of the week – a midweek pizza, a luxurious weekend treat, a light lunch or a leisurely brunch. With live music and space for private functions in the stunning room upstairs, Chime has created a space that caters for all the local community.

The produce is selected with care, keeping everything local and fresh – the meat, for example, comes from the butcher just a few doors away. The bespoke cocktails are sure to tempt the tastebuds and the well-researched wine list has something for all occasions.

So, just where did it get that name? A little digging in Hartford's historical records reveals that the building – the old village store – is in fact home to a Victorian fire bell, which would have chimed to alert the horse-drawn fire engine which was housed in the neighbouring Red Lion Free House. The original bell actually remains in the premises to this day. From a fascinating past to an exciting future – Chime has brought a new lease of life to one of Hartford's historic buildings.

Chime

WELSH LAMB RUMP WITH WILD MUSHROOMS, PURPLE HAZE CARROTS, PEA PURÉE AND POTATO TERRINE

We source our Welsh lamb from a little butchers in the sleepy village of Hartford. As for the recipe, it's our Head Chef's creation. Very moreish and packed full of flavour! Serves 4

Ingredients

8 Maris Piper potatoes

100g butter, melted, plus a little butter for cooking the mushrooms

35g Parmesan, grated

4 lamb rumps

2 garlic cloves, crushed

1 rosemary sprig

300g wild purple haze carrots or similar

300g frozen peas

200ml water, boiled

300g fresh wild mushrooms

Salt and black pepper

2 baby candied beetroot, thinly sliced, to garnish

Edible flowers, to garnish (optional)

Method

Prepare the terrine the day before. Preheat the oven to 180°C. Peel, square and thinly slice the potatoes using a mandoline. Brush the base and sides of a loaf tin with melted butter, and arrange a layer of the potato slices in the base of the tin. Brush the layer with melted butter and sprinkle with Parmesan. Keep building the layers, seasoning as you go. Once completed, cover in tin foil and place in the preheated oven for 1 hour to 1 hour 30 minutes, or until the potatoes are tender throughout. Remove from the oven and set aside for 45 minutes, then press with a similar loaf tin adding a little weight to the top. Leave to chill overnight.

The next day, preheat the oven to 180°C. Start by seasoning the lamb rumps. Place in a hot pan (no oil) fat-side down. Once the fat has started to get a nice even colour, brown the rest of the lamb. Add the crushed garlic and rosemary to the pan for a further 1 minute. Place in the oven for 6-8 minutes.

Remove the terrine from the fridge and carefully remove it from the tin. Cut lengthways into strips with a width of 2cm. Add to the oven for 8-10 minutes. Meanwhile, clean the carrots and blanch in seasoned boiling water until al dente, refresh in ice water to stop the cooking completely.

Now for the pea purée. Add the peas and boiling water to a food processor, and start off processing slowly and building up the speed gradually. Once at maximum speed, blend for 1 minute. Pass the peas through a fine chinois or sieve, and season to taste. Add to a small saucepan ready to reheat and serve.

Remove the lamb from the oven. Leave to rest for 3-4 minutes with a plate over the top to retain the heat. Sauté the wild mushrooms with a little butter and season. Bring the carrots up to heat along with the pea purée.

Now to plate. Carve your lamb. Arrange the wild mushrooms in a strip along the plate. Lay your terrine lengthways alongside the mushrooms. Place your carrots at one end of the plate and lay the lamb over. At the opposite side to your lamb, dot the pea purée generously. Garnish with very thinly sliced candied beetroot and, if you can get your hands on some, beautifully coloured edible flowers.

A Unique Dining EXPERIENCE

Set within the grounds of HMP Styal's women's prison, The Clink Restaurant offers an innovative dining experience like no other.

There is something unexpected happening in the grounds of HMP Styal which is original, creative and utterly delicious. The beautiful new restaurant, where the cooking and service is done by 30 women prisoners who are participating in a rehabilitative training scheme, is offering high-end dining in a unique environment.

The restaurant opened its doors in April 2015 and already has The Sustainable Restaurant Association's 3-star Award under its belt. Locally-sourced and seasonal produce is transformed into mouth-watering dishes using the latest cooking techniques. From seafood terrine layered with scallops, horseradish emulsion and beetroot crisps to sesame-coated duck breast, bok choy and julienne of vegetables in an Asian-style broth and served with sticky rice, the menu is composed of classic dishes with modern twists.

The two private dining rooms seat 10 and 20 people and offer plasma screens if required – ideal for making a business lunch more memorable. There is also the option for private venue hire including evenings and weekends.

The original concept of The Clink Restaurant was created by Alberto Crisci when he recognised the potential of some of the prisoners at HMP High Down who were working in the prison kitchens. In May 2009 the first Clink Restaurant at HMP High Down officially opened as the first public restaurant to open within the walls of a working prison.

The women working in the restaurant are studying towards City & Guilds NVQs in Food Service and Food Preparation, and will be mentored following their release to help them find employment within the hospitality industry. This combination of hands-on training, a recognised qualification and comprehensive mentoring has led to many incredible success stories for women who have been rehabilitated into the community with a new career. It is also a wonderful way to challenge preconceptions and create an unusual dining experience for local residents.

The Clink currently runs a total of four restaurants at prisons in the UK, and together they contribute 150 training positions for prisoners and have accumulated over 30 awards. With the new restaurant at Styal proving to be successful already, there could be plenty more awards to come for this innovative charity.

www.theclinkcharity.org

The Clink Restaurant

TRIO OF APPLE

To make this delicious celebration of the Bramley apple, you will need a sugar thermometer, a piping bag, four dariole moulds and some small lolly pop sticks or cocktail sticks. You'll also need plenty of Bramley apples – perfect for when you have a glut of them to use up. Serves 4

Ingredients

Apple purée:

100ml water

400g Bramley apples, cored and sliced

Apple Mousse:

125g apple purée (see above)

25g sugar

1 leaf bronze gelatine, soaked and drained

125ml double cream

Toffee apples:

140g Bramley apples, peeled and cored

50g caster sugar

100ml water

1ml white wine vinegar

10g Lyle's golden syrup

Chocolate soil:

100g caster sugar

30ml water

70g dark chocolate

To decorate:

Redcurrants and raspberries

An apple and a few strawberries

Edible flowers and micro herbs

Method

For the apple purée, pour the water into a saucepan and add the apples. Bring to the boil and simmer for 5-10 minutes or until the apples are tender. Transfer the mixture to a bowl and mash. The peel will usually separate when you mash the apples manually – just take it out to avoid a chunky texture in your purée. (If you use a blender or electric masher, there is no need to separate the peel, as it will be mashed to a creamy consistency). Continue to mash until the apple is creamy.

For the apple mousse, put apple purée into a saucepan with the sugar. Add the soaked and drained gelatine and whisk until the gelatine has dissolved. Allow to cool to room temperature. Whip the cream. Add the cooled apple purée mixture to the cream and fold in gently until incorporated. Place the mousse into a piping bag and pipe into four dariole moulds. Allow to set in the refrigerator for 5 hours.

For the toffee apples, use a melon baller to create balls of apple. Stick a small lolly pop stick or cocktail stick into each ball. Lay out a sheet of baking parchment and place the apple balls on this, close to your stovetop. Tip the sugar into a saucepan along with the water and set over a medium heat. Cook for 5 minutes until the sugar dissolves. Stir in the vinegar and golden syrup. Set a sugar thermometer in the pan and boil to 150°C. If you don't have a thermometer, you can test the toffee by pouring a little into a bowl of cold water. It should harden instantly and, when removed, be brittle and easy to break. If you can still squish the toffee, continue to boil it. Working quickly and very carefully, dip and twist each apple in the hot toffee until covered, let any excess drip away, then place on the baking parchment to harden. You may have to heat the toffee a little if the temperature drops and it starts to feel thick and viscous.

For the chocolate soil, heat the sugar and water in a saucepan to 130°C using a sugar thermometer. As soon as it reaches this temperature, add the chocolate and whisk. Stir for 2 minutes until dries out and breaks up.

To plate up, place the chocolate soil on a plate (or in wooden box). Place the apple mousse on top of chocolate soil. Add the toffee apples. Use redcurrants and raspberries to decorate, scattering them around. Use a Paris scoop to ball an apple and some strawberries and scatter these around. Add some edible flowers and micro herbs.

DeFining WINE

The experts and wine-lovers at DeFINE Food & Wine want to let us all in on a few secrets when it comes to the wonderful, magical and sometimes downright daunting world of wine...

There is something a little unusual about DeFINE Food & Wine. In fact they are pretty sure that they are like no other wine store you've ever visited. They are one of the country's leading independent wine merchants, but with the warm and friendly atmosphere of a local shop.

Named as Regional Merchant of the Year for the North-West in the International Wine Challenge, they are true wine specialists and it's safe to say there is very little they don't know about it – they taste thousands of wines each year to make sure their shelves are filled with the very best bottles. They have been established on the main Chester Road in Sandiway since the turn of the millennium, but the excitement still bubbles like the finest Champagne – whether you're asking about the world's finest vintages or a great-tasting tipple to go with a pizza.

On one hand, they proudly supply wine to Michelin-star restaurants such as The Waterside and Restaurant Gordon Ramsay, yet on the other, they offer a great value Pinot Grigio to Mrs Booth on Norley Road! They also have a successful website and international mail order service and are dedicated to promoting decent, honest wine to discerning Cheshire mouths, offering expert advice to help you find wines to suit your wallet, your palate and your gullet.

Owner Jon explains how their approach isn't to 'demystify' wine, as is so often claimed by independent retailers: "Wine is, or can be, mystical, magical and mind-altering. Our goal is to tell the tale behind the label and bring the liquid to life." They want us all to feel at home exploring the world of wine, and with a bit of help from their Enomatic machines, can offer an ever-changing range of 32 wines for you to try before you buy.

Of course, it's not just wine – the deli is stocked with over 50 cheeses, including artisan British products and some of the finest European offerings, as well as utterly delicious Tuscan and Spanish sausages, cured meats and olives. Finest-quality speciality food from around the world includes such delights as Musetti coffee, Benedetto Cavalieri pasta and Ortiz Bonito tuna. And with plans for expansion underway, it looks like there will be lots of exciting developments to come in the future...

DeFINE Food & Wine
PENNE WITH TUSCAN SAUSAGE

A visit to DeFINE to pick up delicious Tuscan sausages, smoked pancetta, Sardinian chopped tomatoes, Benedetto Cavalieri penne and a bottle of red wine and you can whip up a simple yet flavour-packed pasta dish. Serves 4

Ingredients

1 pack of Define's Tuscan Sausage with fennel (6 sausages)

75g of Define's smoked pancetta, diced

1 medium onion, diced

1 carrot, diced

1 stick of celery, diced

1 clove of garlic, crushed

Chilli flakes (optional)

125ml Nero d'Avola or other red wine

1 tin of Define's Sardinian chopped tomatoes

400g Define's Benedetto Cavalieri penne

A few drops of extra virgin olive oil

150ml full-fat crème fraiche

75g grated Parmesan

Handful of flat leaf parsley, chopped

Olive oil, for cooking

Salt and ground black pepper

Method

Remove the sausage from the skins (I slice them in half lengthways without cutting through the underside of the skin, then fold them out from their skins) and break into small chunks using your fingers.

In a heavy-based pan, fry the pancetta until crisp and golden, then remove from the pan. Soften the onion, carrot and celery over a gentle heat for 5 minutes in a couple of tablespoons of olive oil, until soft. Add the garlic and a few chilli flakes if you like a bit of heat, turn the heat up and fry for another minute. Remove the contents from the pan. Turn up the heat and, when hot, throw in the sausage pieces. Don't stir it for a few minutes (you want the sausage to brown a bit), then stir, and leave again for a couple of minutes.

Return the ingredients removed earlier to the pan and add the wine. Boil for a few minutes to boil off the alcohol. Drink some wine whilst you're cooking, so you're not too upset about boiling off the alcohol. Add the tin of tomatoes and give it all a good stir, add a good few twists of black pepper and leave it all to bubble away very gently for a good half hour, or up to an hour if you've got time, stirring regularly.

Bring a large pan of water to the boil and cook the penne to your desired texture. Towards the end of cooking, add a few tablespoons of the pasta water to the sausage sauce to loosen it up a bit. Drain the pasta and stir through a few drops of extra virgin olive oil.

When you're ready to serve, stir the crème fraîche and the grated Parmesan through the sauce. Check for seasoning – you probably won't need to add any salt. Stir through some chopped parsley and serve the sauce spooned on top of the penne.

Totally DELI-CIOUS

A foodie destination for Hoole residents and curious tourists alike,
Deli-vert is a Chester favourite known for bringing together fine foods
from Cheshire and beyond.

Nestled in the historic streets of Hoole in Chester, the small delicatessen is famous locally for its charming character and friendly atmosphere. It welcomes hungry tourists during the busy summer months with the same charming hospitality it gives its regulars, many of whom are known by name. Set amongst a plethora of other independent businesses, Deli-vert is part of an inspiring community with a village feel, where people are keen to support small traders, unique shops and local produce.

Simon and his partner Andy took over the deli in 2014 and have been blown away by the support of the locals. After a career working in finance, insurance and banking, Simon had been dreaming of setting up his own foodie business for years. When the opportunity arose in the heart of Hoole to turn his ambitions into reality, he took the plunge… and he certainly hasn't looked back.

Scooping awards for Cheshire's Best Deli in 2014 and 2015 at the Taste Cheshire Food and Drink Awards, along with Best Sandwich Shop in Cheshire, it's fair to say Simon has hit the ground running. He is passionate about local produce as well as sourcing the best ingredients from around the world. The aim at Deli-vert is for 50% of their stock to be sourced from within 50 miles of the shop, and the remaining 50% is selected from the UK's finest offerings and Europe's world-famous produce.

For Simon, being able to support small-scale local producers is what makes the shop so special. He loves the amazing variety of produce he can bring together under one roof. Fresh salads and sandwiches are made to order, and the homemade quiches and famous sausage rolls are made fresh on-site each day. From local artisan chutneys and Cheshire cheeses to Italian olives and the finest French Camembert, the selection of mouth-watering goodies is always changing. What remains the same is the commitment to the finest quality food and old-fashioned friendly service.

Deli-vert

deli-vert
Fine foods from cheshire and beyond...

'Buy Local' Food Award 2009
WINNER

Chester Food & Drink Festival
2008
WINNER
Gold Award
Local Produce Shop

Deli-vert
CHESHIRE CHEESE QUICHE WITH PEPPERS ACCOMPANIED BY A FRESH CITRUS SALAD

Our popular quiche made with local Cheshire cheese is served with a zingy salad.

Serves 6

Ingredients

Pastry:

450g plain flour

200g salted butter diced

A pinch of salt

Water

Quiche filling:

7 free-range eggs

50ml whole milk

100g Cheshire cheese, grated

1 green, 1 red and 1 yellow bell pepper, diced

Salad:

100g Brazil nuts lightly chopped

40g pine nuts

Fresh salad leaves

24 baby tomatoes halved

150g pomelo flesh

50g Cheshire cheese, crumbled

Zest of a lemon

Dressing:

60ml orange juice

20ml extra virgin olive oil

A pinch of salt

Freshly ground black pepper

Method

In a large bowl mix together the flour and butter with your fingers until it resembles breadcrumbs. Add the salt and enough water to just bring the mixture together. Knead the dough for 2 minutes on a floured board, wrap in cling film and leave in the fridge for 20 minutes to chill. Alternatively purchase individual savoury tart cases of approximately 10cm in diameter preferably uncooked.

Preheat the oven to 180°C. For the quiche filling, mix together the eggs and milk in a jug and set aside.

Roll out the pastry, cut into discs and place into buttered loose-bottomed 10cm tart cases ready for the filling. In the base sprinkle 80% of the grated cheese, which will prevent the bottom from going soggy, split the diced peppers evenly between each tart, sprinkle over the remaining cheese and fill to the top with the egg mixture.

Bake in the preheated oven for 25 minutes, or until they have set and started to take on some light colour.

Lightly toast the nuts in a dry pan for a few moments until the pine nuts start to take a little colour, but be careful not to burn. Put the remaining salad ingredients in a large bowl, top with the nuts and sprinkle with a chiffonade of the lemon zest.

Combine all the ingredients for the dressing, mix vigorously, then dress the leaves generously.

The quiche can be served hot or cold.

Country pub TRADITIONS

The Egerton Arms in Chelford is a family-run pub that is steeped in local history and cherished by the community thanks to its outstanding locally-sourced food.

Characterful low beams, unusual antiques on display, the long bar with old brass pumps and age-old fireplaces are a reminder that The Egerton Arms has been feeding and watering people in Chelford since the 16th century – a coach house and pub where gentry and royals would freshen up on their way to visiting Lord Egerton's estate at nearby Tatton Park, staff and horse groomers would stay at The Egerton Arms while their masters were away.

Today it has been brought back to life with love and care by owners Jeremy Hague and Anne Lefeuvre – extended and repaired so that it remains true to its heritage while shining as a modern restaurant and thoroughly welcoming pub. Jeremy and Anne have 30 years of experience in the restaurant trade and family connections to the farming community.

Their focus on good food and welcoming families is clear in everything they do. The Sunday roasts are famous throughout the area – raved about on Trip Advisor as the best people have ever tasted. Families return time after time to enjoy the surroundings, won over by the informal atmosphere and the ease at which they can enjoy thoroughly good food in a relaxing setting. There's a lovely kids' play area outside, a reasonably priced children's menu, large family tables with space to put the buggy and it's dog-friendly, too, of course.

Just as he is always expanding and regenerating the pub, Jeremy does the same for the food and events – have a look at the events board as you walk in or check the website to see what is coming up. From 'pie and a pint week' to 'mussels and chips night', the tables are always packed with families enjoying the food and atmosphere. Gluten-free options pepper the menu, making them one of Cheshire's most popular pub-restaurants for those with gluten-intolerance.

Next door, the commitment to good food is showcased in the adjoining Jones Deli. If you've eaten an amazing dish in the pub, chances are you might be able to buy some of the ingredients in the deli. From local Cheshire beers and homemade Scotch eggs to the finest oils and vinegars, the mouth-watering display is testament to the love of food that Jeremy and Anne share. With a terrace outside, it's an ideal spot to enjoy breakfast and a coffee in the sunshine, too.

The Egerton Arms and Jones Deli
STUFFED BLACK PUDDING BALLS WITH MUSTARD SAUCE

A popular pub snack that is easy to make at home using ingredients
from Jones Deli. Serves 2

Ingredients

A wedge of Brie (or Camembert)

200g black pudding

100g plain flour, for coating

2 eggs, whisked, for coating

200g Panko breadcrumbs, for coating

4 small slices of lean streaky bacon

300ml double cream

2 tbsp English mustard

2 tbsp wholegrain mustard

Parsley or pea shoots, to garnish

Method

First make four individual one-inch Brie balls. Mould the black pudding around the Brie balls by hand, season with a little salt and pepper and herbs (thyme in this recipe) – the balls should now be about 2 inches round (like a golf ball).

Place the flour in one bowl, the beaten eggs in another bowl and the Panko breadcrumbs in a third bowl. Season the breadcrumbs. Coat the balls lightly in the flour and dip into the whisked egg wash. Roll heavily (to get a good coating) in the seasoned Panko breadcrumbs.

Deep-fry the balls at 180°C for 2-3 minutes, then drain on kitchen paper. (Or you can crisp up in a pan over a medium heat until golden all over and then finish in the oven for 3 minutes.) Try not to overcook the balls as the cheese will spill out.

Fry the streaky bacon to a firm crisp finish and dry with kitchen paper.

In a pan, heat the cream, English mustard and wholegrain mustard together. Bring the cream mustard sauce gently to boil and add extra mustard to taste.

Plate up the balls on a plate of choice, pour the sauce over generously, add the bacon slices criss-crossed on the balls and a light garnish of parsley, or pea shoots as shown.

affordable LUXURY

Seasonal produce, local suppliers and skilful cooking in the restaurant's open kitchen – The Fat Loaf in Sale has become a local favourite thanks to its commitment to fresh cooking, excellent service and welcoming atmosphere.

On the outskirts of Manchester, nestled on the bustling high street of Ashton-on-Mersey, The Fat Loaf is a restaurant that is adored by the local community for its welcoming atmosphere, honest pricing and commitment to local, seasonal ingredients. A firm favourite across Sale and the south Manchester area, this local gem has acquired a loyal following of regulars.

In the summer, the bi-folding windows open the restaurant interior to the outdoors and there is also space for alfresco dining. The open kitchen captures the eye of the diners as they can watch the chefs prepare their meals in front of their eyes, showing the fresh, local ingredients being transformed into mouth-watering plates. The skilful chefs have been known to hand out a few recipe tips to curious diners, too!

The commitment to happy customers is revealed in the reviews from Sale residents who return to The Fat Loaf regularly. With options such as bring your own wine nights and a fixed-price lunch and early evening menu, the restaurant caters for midweek meals that won't break the bank. The aim is to make "eating out affordable enough to become a weekday habit… not just a weekend treat."

However, what makes them stand out from the crowd is the quality. Eating at The Fat Loaf is an affordable luxury. With suppliers including Frost Butchers of Chorlton for meat, Manchester Veg People for local vegetables and Abbey Lees Farm for free-range eggs, there is no compromise on the finest seasonal ingredients.

The menu showcases British classics peppered with modern twists and a dash of flavour inspiration from around the world – a selection of small plates will whet the appetite with Morcambe Bay shrimps with watercress, cayenne and mace butter and a warm English muffin… or braised pig's cheeks with chilli, ginger, mandarins, shallots and crispy cabbage… or buttermilk fried chicken with Singapore chilli sauce and shredded vegetables. For mains, think king prawn linguine, grilled seabass or Goosnagh duck breast… or opt for a steak cooked to perfection with a classic sauce and a portion of beef dripping chips on the side. What could be better than that?

The Fat Loaf
LAMB RUMP, SLOW-BRAISED STIFADO SAUCE AND CRISPY POTATOES

An amazingly popular dish with our customers, using W. H. Frost Butcher's lamb really gives it a fantastic flavour. It is easy to make at home for a dinner party but definitely has the wow factor. Serves 4

Ingredients

Stifado Sauce:

500g lamb shoulder, diced

125ml extra virgin olive oil

1 large onion, diced

8 garlic cloves, chopped

250ml glass of red wine

3 tbsp red wine vinegar

1 cinnamon stick

4 whole cloves

½–1 tsp ground nutmeg

4 bay leaves

3 sprigs of rosemary

3 tbsp tomato purée

2 tomatoes, chopped

500g shallots

Sea salt and black pepper

Crispy Potatoes:

3 large potatoes, peeled and cut into 1cm dice

4 garlic cloves, sliced

Sea salt

About 100ml olive oil

Lamb Rumps:

4 lamb rumps, 200g each

Method

Start by making the slow-braised stifado sauce. Preheat the oven to 140°C.

Put the diced lamb shoulder in a frying pan and sear on all sides. Remove from the pan and set aside. Add the olive oil, onions and garlic and cook until the onions start to go soft (about 5 minutes). Then add the glass of red wine and the red wine vinegar. Cover and leave to cook for 5 minutes, then add the cinnamon, cloves, nutmeg, bay leaves, rosemary, tomato purée and salt and pepper to taste. Keep stirring to let all the ingredients mix together. Finally add the chopped tomatoes and continue stirring for 5 minutes. Add the seared lamb back in.

Transfer to a clay pot or casserole dish and add 250-500ml water, being careful not to drown the sauce. Cook for at least 2 hours 30 minutes in the preheated oven, checking it regularly as you don't want it to dry out. Add extra water if needed – you are aiming for a thick, rich sauce.

While the lamb is cooking, place the shallots into hot water to soften the skins, then peel them. Fry the peeled shallots in a little olive oil, being careful not to burn them – just aim to soften them and add a little colour. Add these to the stifado after 1 hour of cooking in the oven.

Once ready, the meat should be tender and can be flaked through the sauce. Remove from the oven and set aside to keep warm. Increase the temperature to 200°C for the crispy potatoes.

To make the crispy potatoes, boil the cubed potatoes in a pan of salted water for about 8 minutes until just cooked. Drain and allow to cool. Add the potatoes to a roasting tray with slices of garlic, sea salt, and a generous glug of olive oil, mix together and roast in the oven for approximately 20 minutes or until golden brown and soft in the middle.

Finally for the lamb rumps, increase the oven temperature to 220°C. Heat an ovenproof frying pan and add the seasoned lamb rumps, seal all over until golden brown. Put into the preheated oven for about 12 minutes. Remove and allow to rest for 4-5 minutes.

To plate, you should first place the stifado in the base of a bowl with plenty of shallots, then slice the lamb rump and arrange on the top. Finally sprinkle the potatoes onto the top and serve.

The Organic GARDEN

The Garden in Hale is an organic café serving up earth-friendly food, full of flavour and designed to nourish the body from the inside out.

Set in the leafy streets of Hale, The Garden is a café where life is celebrated through food. Amy and Kate, the co-owners, had been friends for years. Although Amy had always worked in the hospitality industry, Kate had been a primary school teacher and had found her health had suffered due to the stresses of everyday life. After discovering a love for yoga, Kate became aware of how she could take control of her own health through her diet and lifestyle.

Amy's interest in healthy food developed after her father was diagnosed with a terminal illness and she began learning about natural medicine through diet. Motivated to show people just how tasty health-giving food could be, Kate and Amy decided to put their passion into a joint venture, and The Garden was born.

The dishes that come out of the kitchen are vibrant and beautiful, packed with nutrition and flavour. The ingredients are local and seasonal, which, as described by The Garden, is nature's way of giving your body the right nutrients it needs at each time of year. By choosing to support local suppliers, The Garden hope to do their part in reducing 'food miles'.

They have a special interest in the alkaline diet and can provide alkaline ratings for food if customers are interested, which is something they love to do – educating and inspiring people about food is a big part of Kate and Amy's passion for the restaurant. However, it is the deliciously irresistible flavours as well as the health benefits that keep people coming back time and time again!

The menu is mainly vegan with some vegetarian offerings dotted throughout. There is the option to add sustainable, organic and ethically sourced meat or fish to any dish too. The idea is it turns the usual restaurant menu on its head – making meat the option rather than the rule. Much of the menu is naturally gluten and dairy-free, so for those with intolerances to gluten or lactose The Garden has become a favourite venue, as they know they can choose almost anything off the menu and it will suit their dietary needs.

Whatever your diet, pop in and speak to the knowledgeable staff and they'll do their best to suggest something suitable. Or even if you just fancy a healthy lunch, a superfood-packed juice, a surprisingly healthy (but delicious) cake or a soothing cup of loose-leaf tea – it's a place to sit back, relax and treat yourself to truly restorative nourishment in a charming local restaurant.

The Garden

The Garden

LENTIL BURGERS

A firm favourite from our 2015 spring/summer menu, our hugely popular lentil burger charmed our customers with its flexible offerings – catering for gluten-free, dairy-free and vegan diets as well as being super healthy and totally delish!

Serves 6

Ingredients

2 onions, diced
1 garlic clove, minced
250g chestnut mushrooms, diced
1 tbsp coconut oil
200g raw spinach
Juice of 2 lemons
1 tsp cumin
1 vegetable stock cube
250g gluten-free breadcrumbs
400g green lentils, cooked
A pinch of Himalayan pink salt
Black pepper

Method

Preheat the oven to 180°C.

Sauté the onions, garlic and mushrooms in the coconut oil over medium heat for 5-10 minutes until golden brown. Add the spinach and stir until wilted. Add the lemon juice, cumin and stock and simmer over medium heat for 5 minutes more.

Blend in a food processor then add the breadcrumbs and lentils. Season with the Himalayan pink salt and black pepper. Pour the mixture into a mixing bowl then shape into six burger patties.

Place on a baking tray and cook in the preheated oven for 40 minutes.

Britain's best
PIE MAKER?

Winners in nine categories at the British Pie Awards as well as having the prestigious title of North West Fine Food Producer of the Year in a competition judged by the Great British Menu Winner, Nigel Haworth, Great North Pie Co is earning a reputation as one of Britain's best pie makers.

Neil has always been a keen food-lover and ambitious home-cook. His journey to pie making started purely as a hobby whilst serving as an officer in The Greater Manchester Police. Creating Great North Pie Co did not just happen overnight; it was born from Neil's passion for food in his home kitchen with every aspect of the pie, from pastry to filling, being carefully thought out, tasted and tweaked until he had recipes he was happy with.

The pies are made with all-butter pastry in custom-made pie tins to create the perfect pies, making it easy to see why the pies have achieved such acclaim. Neil and Sarah like to create unique flavour combinations for their pies, mixing up simple classics in modern ways, such as their steak & stout pie – Cheshire beef, stout, roast onion purée, carrots roasted with cinnamon and star anise, redcurrant jelly, Worcestershire sauce, black pepper, mustard and onion seeds.

There is no set menu – Neil focuses on quality, making use of the best of Cheshire and its neighbouring counties' incredible ingredients. He is constantly researching new ingredients and cooking techniques to ensure that Great North Pie Co continue to produce something that little bit different. Rest assured though you can still be sure to find classic flavours and these flavours are wowing diners and awards panels alike. Their Goosnargh chicken & mushroom with English mustard & tarragon secured the title Supreme Champion of the British Pie Awards 2015.

In fact they swept the board in 2015, with Best Chicken Pie, Best Vegetarian Pie (saag paneer), Best Beef Pie (minced beef and bovril) and Best Fish Pie (smoked eel, apple, potato cream, horseradish and garlic). The fish pie holds a special place in their hearts and they have shared the recipe overleaf. It looks like Great North Pie Co may need a bigger award cabinet… Other accolades include the title of Best Pie in Britain, as well as Small Producer of the Year.

Neil and Sarah have no plans to become the biggest pie company in the world, instead they aim to be one of the best.

Great North Pie Co.
SMOKED EEL PIE WITH APPLE, POTATO AND HORSERADISH CREAM CHESTNUT FLOUR PASTRY

Before we started the business we would go down to London and end up in one of the old traditional pie and mash shops selling pie, mash and liquor with jellied eels. Years later when we started thinking about ideas for a fish pie, it just seemed like a good idea to replace the jellied eel with smoked eel. We made a version of this in 2011 and it won Best Fish pie in Britain at the 2011 British Pie Awards. We played about with the recipe and it won again in 2015. Eel is not to everyone's taste but it does appeal to a lot of food lovers looking for something different. Smoked mackerel also works well. Serves 4

Ingredients

Chestnut flour pastry:

500g plain flour

50g chestnut flour

A pinch of salt

250g butter

1 egg

150ml iced water

Filling:

200g smoked eel

1 pink lady apple, peeled and cored

½ lemon

A handful of roughly chopped flat leaf parsley

Potato and horseradish cream:

250g cooked potato

100ml potato cooking water

125g single cream

35g extra virgin olive oil

½ tsp salt

1½ tsp creamed horseradish

½ clove garlic, finely grated

Topping:

Panko breadcrumbs

Poppy seeds

Caraway seeds

Egg for glaze

Method

For the pastry, put the flours, salt and butter in a food processor and blend into fine breadcrumbs. Add the egg and blitz into the pastry. Gradually add the water, a little at a time, blending on medium speed until the mixture binds together and becomes smooth – you may not need all the water. Remove the dough, wrap it in clingfilm and place in the fridge to rest for an hour

For the filling, dice the smoked eel into 1cm squares or shred into small pieces. Dice the apples into pieces a little smaller than the eel. Squeeze over some lemon juice to stop it from discolouring.

To make the potato cream, blend the cooked potatoes with the potato cooking water. Add the single cream, extra virgin olive oil, salt, horseradish and garlic, then blend again until smooth. Place in the fridge and chill.

Mix the smoked eel with the diced apple and a handful of roughly chopped parsley. Mix through 400g of the potato cream to help bind the mixture and carefully fold through.

Preheat the oven to 180°C. Roll out the pastry to the thickness of a £1 coin and cut into a circle just larger than your tin, making sure it is large enough to line all the way up the sides. Line the tin with the pastry, hanging the edges over the sides. Roll another piece of pastry to the same thickness to use for the lid and trim into a circle just larger than your pie tin.

Fill the pie with the mixture and gently spread down with the back of a spoon. Brush the top edges of the pie with a beaten egg and place the lid on top. Go around the tin gently squeezing the pastry lid to the pastry underneath. Take a floored rolling pin and roll against the sides of the tin to trim off the excess pastry.

Brush the top of the pie with an egg glaze, and sprinkle with panko breadcrumbs, poppy seeds and caraway seeds. Pierce a small hole in the top of the pie and place on a baking tray. Bake in the preheated oven for 18-20 minutes until the pie is nicely coloured on top and the base is crisp. The pie can be eaten straightaway or cooled on a wire rack to be reheated.

A View to DINE FOR

The rolling hills of The Peak District provide the spectacular backdrop to the historic 17th century inn, The Hanging Gate.

Not only is The Hanging Gate the highest pub in Cheshire, it is the fourth highest in England, standing proudly 1100ft above sea level at Higher Sutton near Macclesfield. The views it commands across the valley, as far as Jodrell bank, have helped to earn The Hanging Gate a well-deserved reputation as a stunning destination pub.

It was taken over by Ernst van Zyl, Chef Patron of Michelin-listed The Lord Clyde, when the brewery approached them having dined at their award-winning gastro pub. They took the reins in October 2015, having been won over by its money-can't buy views, and set about putting in lots of hard work to make the most of the breath-taking setting and charming building.

Famous for his relaxed approach to top-quality dining, Ernst was just the man to breathe new life into the kitchens at The Hanging Gate. The menu is a delectable selection of locally-sourced ingredients put together into classic dishes and creative modern plates. From roasted chicken breast, potato purée, heritage carrots and a thyme chicken jus to pan-fried king scallop, black pudding and apple tart, Parma ham and dill oil, the menu offers delicious pub fare that is cooked to the highest standards.

During the summer, dining al fresco is a must to make the most of the magical outlook – there is no better place to watch the sunset in Cheshire, that's for sure. It is no wonder it is such a popular spot for people to enjoy a post-walk pint after a ramble in the local countryside and to refuel with a home-cooked meal.

Since Sarah and Ernst took over in October 2015 and injected their passion for good food and top-notch hospitality, the reputation of this delightful country pub is already spreading far and wide.

The Hanging Gate

LAMB RUMP, SPICED KOFTA SAUSAGE, CAULIFLOWER AND RED CABBAGE

Serves four

Ingredients

4 lamb rump

4 mini lamb kofta sausages

Olive oil

A sprig of thyme

Red cabbage purée:

450g sliced red cabbage

80g red wine

30g red wine vinegar

20g English Mustard

15g sugar

A pinch of salt

½ tsp xanthan powder

Dried red cabbage leaves:

2 red cabbage leaves

Cauliflower purée:

1 head of cauliflower, broken into florets

Milk, as needed

Salt, to season

½ tsp xanthan powder

Cauliflower crisps:

8 large cauliflower florets

Method

To serve:

Place the lamb rump and sausages in a bag with a touch of olive oil and a sprig of thyme. Water bath at 65°C for 35 minutes. Remove and drop into an ice bath to stop the cooking process.

For the red cabbage purée, combine the red cabbage, red wine and red wine vinegar in a bag and seal in a vacuum. Drop in simmering water and cook for 2-3 hours. Empty the contents into a Vitamix or Thermomix and add the English mustard and sugar. Blend until smooth, add a pinch of salt to taste and the xanthan powder to bring it all together to ensure a smooth purée.

For the dried red cabbage leaves, cut the red cabbage leaves into squares of roughly 6cm by 6cm and blanch in simmering water for 10-15 minutes, until the leaves are soft. Drain and dehydrate in an oven or dehydrator at 60°C for 4-5 hours or until crispy.

For the cauliflower purée, place the cauliflower florets into a bag and vacuum. Drop in simmering water for 10-12 minutes, before the cauliflower browns but ensuring it is soft. Empty into a Vitamix or Thermomix and blend with enough milk for a smooth purée. Season with salt and add the xanthan powder to bring the purée together.

For the cauliflower crisps, slice the cauliflower florets on a thick enough cross-section to be presentable and dehydrate for 3-4 hours at 60°C.

To serve, drop the lamb and sausage in a water bath at 58°C for 25 minutes. Remove from the bag and allow the meat to rest for 5 minutes. Season the meat and coat in a thin layer of oil. Fry at a medium heat in a frying pan with butter until the fat and flesh is golden brown. Leave to rest somewhere warm.

Meanwhile parboil two florets of cauliflower per portion for 3 minutes, drain and then deep-fry until golden at 170°C. Season and slice the largest floret through the middle to contrast the white and golden colours of the vegetable. Heat the separate purées.

Arrange the purées and cauliflower on the plate, slice the lamb and sausage in half and sit in the middle of the plate. Garnish with the dried red cabbage and the cauliflower crisps. Finish with Jus. Winner.

It's Plain TO SEE

Perched on a hillside overlooking Cheshire is an award-winning cookery school, an award-winning chef and a very warm welcome.

With 30 years' experience, award-winning Chef Brian Mellor is passionate about passing on skills and knowledge. He opened his cookery school in 2011 in the Grade II listed old Harthill Village School, which he stumbled upon following a festival appearance. Just south of Chester, nestled alongside the Peckforton Hills and with views right across the county, it was the tranquil, rural setting that won him over. These days, as he puts it, it's where he and his friends can pass on their tips, techniques and stories from lives spent in professional kitchens.

The location has given Brian and his partner Mary endless opportunities to make the most of the environment. As well as their fantastic indoor facilities, they are extremely proud of the outdoor cookery areas, which include a BBQ terrace overlooking the Cheshire plains, a 1.5 metre fire pit and a wood-fired pizza oven.

Such wide-ranging facilities go hand-in-hand with a varied selection of classes and tutors. He has brought together many of his colleagues from his career to create a thriving hub of knowledge.

If you don't fancy getting stuck in just yet, the school hall will host you as a grateful recipient of something tasty via a demonstration or pop-up restaurant from Brian himself or one of their many talented friends.

Mary is passionate about great hospitality and ensuring it is always a worthwhile experience for their guests, together Mary and Brian ensure everyone is relaxed and has a memorable time. There's plenty of laughter with an enjoyable atmosphere but it's all backed up by solid learning.

It has always remained a priority for Brian to keep class sizes small and intimate (typically no bigger than eight) so that everyone gets plenty of input and time to practice. That said, it's not uncommon to have the building throbbing with a team-building event for 50 people working their way through 20 street food dishes. This is just one of the reasons why Harthill Cookery School holds the title of Britain's Best Small Cookery School – something that Brian and his team are incredibly proud of.

CHESTER BUNS WITH POTTED CHESHIRE CHEESE AND HARTHILL DAMSON JELLY

Traditionally Chester buns contain mixed spice and are brushed with a sugar glaze – we've adapted it slightly so this rich dough complements the tang of the cheese. It's served with our own jelly made from damsons grown at the school.

Serves 4

Ingredients

50g butter, in small cubes

250g white bread flour

A pinch of salt

1 egg

90ml condensed milk

45ml warm water

15g caster sugar

1 sachet fast-acting yeast

Harthill Damson jelly, to serve

Potted Cheshire cheese:

225g white Cheshire cheese

80ml whole milk

75g cream cheese

1 tsp English mustard

10g chives

A pinch of paprika (optional)

Salt and pepper

Method

Rub the butter into the flour and stir in the salt. Beat the egg in a small bowl. Warm the condensed milk with the water and sugar – it should be no hotter than body temperature, i.e. tepid. Tip the flour mix onto a clean dry work surface, sprinkle the sachet of yeast over the flour and make a well in the centre. (TIP – make it wide and shallow as opposed to like a volcano and you'll have more room to work).

Pour the warm milk mixture into the well, followed by half of the beaten egg (the other half of the egg will be used to glaze the tops later). Mix into a soft dough and knead for 10 minutes. Don't worry if the dough is slightly tacky, it's better at this stage if it's that bit wetter. Cover and leave in a warm place to rise for 2 hours.

When it is ready, knock it back (this is to evenly distribute the gas the yeast has produced). Weigh the dough into 60g pieces then mould them into buns and put them on a greased baking sheet to prove. Cover loosely with oiled cling film until they start to rise.

Preheat the oven to 200°C/400°F/Gas 6. Brush the buns with the remaining half of egg. Bake for about 20 minutes until well risen and golden brown. (Don't worry if you appear not to get too much of a rise to begin with – you'll get a final burst of energy from the yeast in the oven).

For the potted Cheshire Cheese, crumble or process the Cheshire cheese into small pieces and place in a pan with the milk and cream cheese. Gently heat the milk to melt the cheeses together then place in a blender, add the mustard and blend to make the mix smoother. Pour into a bowl and stir it as it cools.

In the meantime chop the chives finely and, only when the cheese is tepid, stir in the chives so that they keep their colour. Taste and season with salt and pepper if needed.

Divide the cheese into four pots or ramekins, cover and chill overnight. Before serving, sprinkle with the paprika if using and serve with warmed Chester buns and some Harthill Damson Jelly.

Harthill Cookery School
SPOTTED DICK AND THICK CUSTARD

The cookery school is situated in the old village primary school where traditional puddings would have been enthusiastically consumed over the centuries, so this recipe is perfect for our setting! Serves 4

Ingredients

Spotted Dick:

100g self-raising flour

A pinch of salt

50g suet

75g currants

30g caster sugar

½ lemon

½ orange

60ml milk

Thick custard:

250ml whole milk

½ tsp vanilla extract

2 egg yolks

50g caster sugar

1 tbsp cornflour

Method

Sift the flour and salt into a bowl. Add the suet, currants and sugar, then finely grate the zest of half a lemon and half an orange into the mix. Pour in the milk and mix to a firm but moist dough (add a little extra milk or flour if necessary to reach the right consistency).

Butter four pudding basins or dariole moulds and fill with the mixture to just over half way up. Place a damp piece of greaseproof paper over each one, making sure it overlaps the edges, and place an elastic band over the top to hold in place.

Using a steamer or a rack over simmering water, add the puddings, cover with a lid or foil and steam for 40 minutes. Top up the pan with water from time to time. (Alternatively you could shape the pudding into a fat roll about 10cm long or a large pudding basin and cook for 1½ hours).

For the custard, warm the milk with the vanilla extract in a saucepan, in the meantime blend yolks and sugar in a bowl, then stir in the cornflour to make a paste. Pour the warmed (not boiled) milk onto the yolk mixture stirring continuously. Return the mix to the pan. Gently heat through on the stove, stirring steadily with a heatproof spatula until the sauce thickens and is smooth. Use additional milk to adjust the consistency as required.

Remove the pudding from the steamer and allow to cool slightly before unwrapping. Serve hot with custard.

A Cut ABOVE

A trusted family-run butchers and bakers, H. E. Coward has been at the heart of Frodsham since 1929, supplying the finest cuts of meat alongside Sue Coward's famous homemade pies.

The Coward family butchers and bakers was established when Mabel Ford of Ford's family butchers married master butcher Harold Edward Coward. Back then the original shop was a 1645 building with its own working abattoir and outbuildings. Due to expansion in 1975 the new, larger and now existing shop was built on site but sadly Harold died just before it was finished and never saw the new shop. It was then that his son Robert naturally took over the reins with his young wife Sue.

Today, in their 40th year of marriage and business, Robert and Sue have worked passionately to make Cowards what it is today. They now work with their daughters Elly and Vicki and more than 30 loyal staff, including Master Butcher Sue Winders and Head Baker Elaine Neild who have both worked with the family for over 25 years. A lively and vibrant place to work and visit, the shop is located in the centre of Frodsham's Main Street and the knowledgeable team welcome everyone with a cheerful smile.

The freshness and quality of the meat speaks for itself. Lamb and beef from nearby North Wales are sourced from farms who they have worked alongside for decades, and for the last 9 years Rob has been rearing rare-breed pigs. The counter boasts over 100 fresh meat products daily – all the traditional cuts you would expect, plus hand-prepared products such as a selection of homemade sausages, burgers and ready meals.

What sets H. E Coward apart is that all the meat is aged and butchered on-site from whole carcasses. This traditional practice ensures a full choice of cuts are available at the very best price and with queues regularly stretching outside the doors of the bustling shop, this method certainly appears to work. People travel from far and wide to get their meat from Coward's, thanks to its reputation for outstanding quality and honest service that has been built up over generations.

Sue Coward's homemade pies are renowned not just in Frodsham, but for miles around. In 1985 Sue decided to make a few pies to sell at the shop, and today they sell over 12,000 a week. Incredibly, every single one is still handmade! The traditional bakery produces over 50 different product lines, each one made entirely on-site and baked fresh daily. From the delicious steak pie to the classic pork pie, the recipes are closely guarded – Sue even has her own secret patented pork pie seasoning.

Cowards also enjoy a strong wholesale trade and the meat, together with Sue's pies, can be found on the menu at many good pubs, restaurants and delis in Cheshire.

H. E. Coward

COWARD'S PIE

HANDMADE HERE
USING OUR
FINEST INGREDIENTS

"They're Delicious"

H.E. Coward Quality Cuts of Meat

H. E. Coward
A PROPER SCOTCH EGG

A tasty yet easy recipe, this is a great way to achieve a soft and bright yolk without the need for deep-frying. But the real secret is our own delicious sausage meat. Serves 1

Ingredients

One extra-large free-range egg

60g traditional H. E Coward pork sausage meat (our pork and tomato sausage meat also makes a nice variation)

Plain flour, to dust

1 extra-large free-range egg, beaten

55ml milk

150g breadcrumbs (we use wholemeal for added flavour)

Method

Place the egg in a pan, cover with cold water, bring to the boil, then take it off the heat and leave to stand for 5 minutes. Remove the egg from the boiled water and immerse it in iced water. Leave to stand for 15 minutes, then peel the egg and set aside.

With wet hands take the sausage meat and pat it out until ½ cm thick. Place the egg in the middle and wrap it around, again with wet hands, smoothing the meat into an even ball ensuring there are no cracks or creases.

Cover with cling film and leave to rest in the fridge, ideally for 20 minutes. Preheat the oven to 190°C.

Sprinkle some flour for dusting in one bowl, mix the beaten egg and milk in another bowl, and place the breadcrumbs in a third bowl. Take the sausage-coated egg and roll it evenly in the flour then the egg wash and finally in the breadcrumbs.

Bake on a rack in the preheated oven for 20 minutes, then serve hot from the oven or allow to cool and served chilled.

H. E. Coward
THE PERFECT ROAST
RIB OF BEEF ON THE BONE

It's all about starting off with the perfect cut. With a beautiful aged rib of beef on the bone, follow this method and you can't go wrong. Guaranteed to be an impressive centre piece on any table. Select your ideal sized rib of beef on the bone – choose from a one-bone rib up to a four-bone – one of our butchers at H. E. Coward's will advise the appropriate size for your meal. Here we are cooking a two-bone rib to generously serve 6 guests.

Ingredients

Roast Rib of Beef:

Rib of beef on the bone (a two-bone rib for 6 people)

Salt and black pepper

Oil, for searing

Good Beefy Gravy:

500g beef bones (chopped by the butcher)

100g plain flour

1 large onion, cut into rings

1 large carrot, halved

250ml red wine

1.5 litres Sue Coward's fresh chicken stock

6 black peppercorns

4 sprigs of thyme

1 bay leaf

2 garlic cloves, halved

Salt, to taste

Method

Roast rib of beef:

Preheat the oven to 160°C. Heat a little oil in a large pan. Season the joint well with salt and pepper. Deeply sear the outside of the joint on all sides until a good caramelisation is achieved.

Place the meat in a roasting tin and cook in the preheated oven for the following times:

18 minutes per 450g for rare.

23 minutes per 450g for medium.

30 minutes per 450g for medium-well to well-done.

Lift out of the oven and leave to rest for 30 minutes, then carve.

Good beefy gravy:

Preheat the oven to 180°C. Roast the bones in a roasting tin in the preheated oven for 45 minutes, then sprinkle over the flour and turn up to 200°C for 15 minutes. In a pan fry off the onion and carrot until caramelised, add the red wine and reduce by one-quarter. Add the roasted bones and stock. Bring to the boil and skim. Add the pepper, thyme, bay and garlic. Bring to the boil and skim again, then reduce to a simmer for 40 minutes. Strain and reduce to your preferred consistency. Season to taste. When your joint has rested pour in the meat juices in to finish your good beefy gravy.

Can I have some CHEESE PLEASE!

The International Cheese Awards is the largest cheese and dairy show in the World. It is held once a year at Dorfold Park, near Nantwich.

The show started in 1897 and continues to grow year on year, attracting over 4,500 entries from across the world. Today it is proud to be the biggest and best cheese and dairy show in the world.

The awards are a two-day event held on the last Tuesday and Wednesday of July. Day one is the judging and trade day, attended by industry participants and press. Approximately 200 judges from the cheese and dairy industry will sample all the entries all hoping to win the Supreme Champion trophy for the best cheese in show overall.

Day two is scheduled to coincide with the Nantwich and South Cheshire Agricultural Show, and attracts over 40,000 visitors. It is a fantastic day out for all the family with plenty to see and do with main ring attractions, displays and of course, loads of cheese to taste and buy.

The renowned Cheese Marquee is a colossal 80,500 sq ft to enable it to hold a world-record number of entries. In 2015 it held 4615 entries from 31 countries and 2016 looks set to be as exciting. It attracts entries from the smallest independent makers right up to some of the world's biggest cheese producers, with all the different varieties available to sample and buy – from creamy and mild to full-flavoured blues, there is something for every cheese-lover.

The marquee is also home to celebrity chefs doing mouth-watering cooking demonstrations for the crowds throughout the day, which are always a show highlight. 2015 saw James Martin, Will Holland, Jonathan Harrison and Sean Wilson sharing culinary tips and delighting fans whilst whipping up dishes live in Le Gruyere Cookery Theatre.

James will be familiar to everyone from BBC1's Saturday Kitchen, whilst Sean has made the move from the cobbles of Coronation Street to the life of a successful cheese maker with the award-winning Saddleworth Cheese Company. Will Holland was awarded a Michelin star in 2009 at the age of just 29 and was the central region champion on the BBC's Great British Menu and is currently Head Chef of the AA Welsh Restaurant of the Year – Coast in Saundersfoot, whilst Jonathan is Chef Patron of the beautiful 17th-century Sandpiper Inn at Leyburn, Yorkshire Life Dining Pub of the Year. Previously we have seen Gino D'Acampo and Jean-Christophe Novelli demonstrating their wonderful skills too.

The International Cheese Awards is an activity of the Nantwich Agricultural Society, a UK-registered charity.

www.internationalcheeseawards.co.uk

International Cheese Awards
WILL HOLLAND'S WELSH RAREBIT

Will Holland, one of the show's regional celebrity chefs, has created the award's very own Welsh rarebit recipe from one our award-winning Swiss cheeses.

Serves 5

Ingredients

500ml stout

45g Gruyère cheese

130g extra mature cheddar cheese

40g unsalted butter

50g plain flour

125ml milk

20g Dijon mustard

7ml Worcestershire sauce

2g salt

1 shake of Tabasco sauce

1 pinch of cayenne pepper

1 pinch of ground nutmeg

1 pinch of paprika

A few twists of black pepper

10 slices sourdough bread

Method

Place the beer in a saucepan and reduce over a high heat until 125ml remains. Leave to one side until required. Finely grate the two cheeses and leave to one side until required.

In a separate saucepan add the butter and melt over a medium heat. Add the flour and cook for 1 minute, stirring continuously. Gradually add the milk and reduced beer. Continue to cook and stir until the sauce has come to the boil. Remove from the heat and add the grated cheeses. Stir vigorously until all the cheese has melted.

Add the remaining ingredients (apart from the bread!) and mix well. Toast one side of the sourdough slices under a hot grill. Turn the sourdough slices over and spread the cheese mix generously on the untoasted side. Return the rarebits to the grill and cook under a low to medium heat until golden brown and bubbling. Serve immediately.

Various serving suggestions include homemade piccalilli (pictured); tomato, shallot and rocket salad; mushroom duxelles and fresh truffle; smoked tomato fondue and balsamic jelly; or burnt leek purée and onion marmalade.

Welcome to the FAMILY

Two farm shops with on-site butchers, coffee shops and luxurious self-catering accommodation – The Hollies Farm Shops celebrate the finest local produce, excellent customer service and good old-fashioned family values.

The word that is most often used to describe The Hollies Farm Shops is 'family'. Firstly it's a family business in the strictest sense – it began life in 1959 when the Cowap family began selling vegetables from a stand on the side of the road with an honesty box for payment. Today, with four generations involved, the business has grown alongside the expanding family. It is managed by siblings Phil, Ed and Sue Cowap, with help from many other family members.

However, you don't have to be a blood relative to be considered part of the tribe here. Every member of the 150-strong dedicated team is part of The Hollies Farm family, and most of the regular customers feel part of the clan too! The shared passion for quality and customer service is palpable at both sites (Little Budworth and Lower Stretton) – it's the vibrant buzz, friendly smiles and warmth of service that keeps customers coming back time and time again.

However the dedication to local produce also plays a part in their success and it has won them plenty of awards, too. If it's not grown by the family (the potatoes, carrots and seasonal vegetables tend to come from a Cowap family farm), it is sourced from a local producer. In fact, the farm shop has grown alongside its neighbouring businesses, nurturing relationships with some suppliers for as long as 25 years!

An award-winning butchery is on-site at both farm shops, where a knowledgeable butcher is always on-hand to guide customers through their choices, as well as explain the provenance of the meat on sale. Sausages and burgers are made on the premises and they've stacked up more awards than we can mention – including England's Best Burger!

The Little Budworth site also boasts a delicatessen offering homemade pies, quiches and home-cooked meats, as well as a whole host of other fresh produce made daily in the kitchen or selected from the finest local makers.

The coffee shop has won its own string of accolades for its excellent customer care and delicious local produce, and the stunning 5-star lodges have been recognised as some of Cheshire's finest self-catering luxury accommodation. All this from a single vegetable stall on the side of the road – the Cowap family put their success down to the family-run ethos and commitment to the very finest quality in everything they offer.

Why not visit them online at www.theholliesfarmshop.co.uk.

The Hollies
SPICY PULLED LAMB SHOULDER

The Hollies' Master Butcher, Andrew Vernon introduced us to his recipe and we've never looked back! A great recipe to enhance the Welsh lamb experience. Andrew often uses this recipe as it's easy to prepare and he can leave the family to tuck in and enjoy: "I love watching the grandchildren tearing at the lamb and enjoying all those flavours." Serves 6

Ingredients

3kg lamb shoulder with bone

6 tbsp Mrs Darlington's Dijon Mustard

2 tbsp pure Cheshire honey

1 tsp cayenne pepper

4 tbsp golden granulated sugar

1 tbsp Demerara sugar

Method

Score the lamb shoulder using a sharp knife.

Create the marinade by mixing the mustard, honey, cayenne pepper and sugars together until they form a paste.

Push the marinade into the cuts on the scored lamb and rub it all over the lamb shoulder.

Place in a roasting tin and place in the fridge overnight ideally. If time doesn't permit, then place in the fridge for at least 2 hours.

Preheat the oven to 180°C. When the oven has reached temperature, turn it down to 140°C and cook for 4-5 hours. Baste the meat with the juices several times during this time.

When the skin is crispy and the meat pulls from the bone, remove it from the oven, and allow it to rest for 15 minutes. Place the lamb on the serving platter and pour over the roasting juices from the roasting tin.

Serve with root vegetables or enjoy on a bread roll with braised red cabbage.

A recipe
FOR SUCCESS

They've put their hearts, souls and first names into their business... and Joseph Benjamin is one of Chester's stand-out eateries.

Run by brothers Joe and Ben Wright, Joseph Benjamin has all the warmth of a small family-run business with the sleek service and creative flair of a high-end restaurant – a balancing act that the brothers have worked incredibly hard to achieve.

For Benjamin, who manages front of house, the key to success is in the simplicity of honest food and drink served with care and attention in a relaxed and welcoming environment. However the restaurant has held a Michelin Bib Gourmand since 2012, so it is clear there is a lot more to Joseph Benjamin than meets the eye.

In fact the restaurant is acclaimed locally in Chester and further afield – you'll find it in The Good Food Guide as well as The Michelin Guide – as one of Cheshire's finest restaurants. Joseph heads up the kitchen and his many years of experience are evident in his culinary creativity, inventive menus and top-quality cooking. From lighter salads and lunchtime specials to the full three-courses 'a la carte', the relaxed atmosphere in the day time is the perfect setting for the unfussy yet incredibly high-quality food that emerges from the kitchen.

On Thursday, Friday and Saturday evenings the independent restaurant offers an evening menu of locally-sourced and seasonally focused dishes that showcase the brothers' commitment to achieving fine dining flavours without the price tag. There is something for everyone on the menu and their simple classics (think delicious Caesar salads, bavette steaks and platters of cured meats) sit comfortably alongside what they fondly term "more inventive, cheffy dishes".

The 'Notable Wine List' was recognised in The Good Food Guide 2016, demonstrating the care and attention that goes into every single aspect of the business. With the new theatre and cultural centre in Chester, they are looking forward to welcoming new customers with interesting pre-theatres menus too.

Joseph Benjamin

CHESHIRE HONEY

Joseph Benjamin
ISLE OF MAN QUEEN SCALLOP WITH GARLIC AND PARSLEY

A recent hit on our menu, these Isle of Man scallops are so beautiful and fresh, and the exquisite flavour of the smaller 'queenies' is to be embraced. Prepared simply and served on the shell, they also provide a bit of wow! If you struggle to get hold of queen scallops, the larger king scallops will work well too, just grill for an extra minute or two. Serves 4

Ingredients

20 Isle of Man queen scallops in half shell

5 slices white bread, crusts removed and ripped into smaller pieces

A handful of parsley leaves

2 tbsp olive oil

2 garlic cloves, crushed

100g butter, softened

Salt and pepper

Lemon juice

Method

Clean the scallops and rinse under cold water, then pat dry with paper towels.

Put the bread and parsley into a food processor and blend to rough breadcrumbs. Add the olive oil and a pinch of salt and pepper.

Mix the garlic with the butter and a little salt and pepper.

Put the scallops on a tray. Put a teaspoon of the garlic butter on each one. Top with a generous sprinkling of the parsley crumb. Cook under a hot grill for approximately 5 minutes until golden brown and the scallop is just cooked.

Serve immediately with a salad of rocket leaves, thinly sliced red onion and a squeeze of lemon juice.

Farm TO FORK

Farm shop, plant centre, café and pick-your-own seasonal fruits and vegetables, Kenyon Hall Farm is a family farm with lots to offer.

For Tod and Barbara Bulmer, Kenyon Hall Farm is not just their family business, it is their family heritage. They took over the farm in 1978, but Tod's family have been working the land here for a staggering 500 years, first as tenants until Tod's grandfather bought the farm in 1919. With such strong links to the land and the county, Tod and Barbara are passionate about keeping the Bulmer family farm as an intrinsic part of the local community.

When Barbara and Tod first took over the sleepy arable farm, they decided to plant the first 2 acres of strawberries and introduce the pick-your-own enterprise. Some herbs followed, from where the plant centre developed, and gradually Kenyon Hall Farm expanded into a thriving foodie destination.

Today the farm is unique in the North-West as its pick-your-own business has expanded to incorporate a whole host of seasonal fruits and vegetables that ripen throughout the summer: strawberries, raspberries and currants from June; garden peas, mangetout and broad beans from July; onions, blackberries and corn from July; right through to pumpkins and squashes in October.

In the café, Barbara always bases her menu around the fresh seasonal produce they have available and her afternoon teas

with homemade cakes are famous. The Manchester Tart recipe overleaf is made using homemade jam from their home-grown raspberries! The pumpkin festival was a real hit in 2015 with people picking and carving their own pumpkins, and tucking into Barbara's delicious pumpkin pie in the café. In fact it was so popular that every single pumpkin on Kenyon Hall Farm was picked!

The eco-friendly farm shop (a mile of pipes heat it from underground!) brings together products from a range of farmers and producers – such as organic meat, free-range chicken and eggs, seasonal fruits and veggies, artisan bread, their own award-winning jams and chutneys, ethically sourced freshly frozen fish, and a range of ales and ciders from local breweries.

For those who would like even more convenience, they offer a unique delivery business Northern Harvest, with 3000 products available online from local producers (www.northernharvest.co.uk). Simply do your shopping on the website and the lovely folk at Kenyon Hall Farm will collect it all together and deliver it to you – there has never been an easier way to shop local!

Kenyon Hall Farm
MANCHESTER TART

This old-fashioned dessert is a winner in our café and has been for four years.
Some of our customers say it reminds them of school. We make it using our
homemade raspberry jam from our home-grown raspberries! Serves 6

Ingredients

Pastry:

340g plain flour

85g lard, cut into small cubes

85g hard margarine, cut into small cubes

Filling:

3 heaped tbsp Kenyon Hall Homemade Raspberry Jam

2 large bananas, sliced

55g custard powder

55g sugar

840ml milk

Topping:

Desiccated coconut

Glacé cherries

Method

Preheat the oven to 200°C (Gas 6).

To make the pastry, put flour into a large mixing bowl (or food processor). Add the cubed fats and rub (or process) the fats into the flour until the mixture resembles breadcrumbs. Add 3 tbsp cold water and bind the mixture to a soft but dry dough; add more water if required. Smooth the dough into a round on a clean, lightly floured surface and roll the pastry out to approximately 2cm larger than the dish all round (we make ours in a 22cm Pyrex flan dish).

Lift the pastry with the rolling pin on to the dish and ease it into the base and up the sides with your fingers, pressing to eliminate air bubbles. Line the pastry case with greaseproof paper and baking beans (or dried peas reserved for this purpose).

Bake in the hot oven for 10-15 minutes until the pastry is golden brown. Remove the baking beans and paper and return the case to the oven until the base is cooked. Allow to cool.

Spread the Kenyon Hall Homemade Raspberry Jam over the base of the pastry and layer the sliced bananas thinly over it.

Put the custard powder and sugar into a jug and blend to a smooth paste with a little of the milk.

Boil the rest of the milk and pour in to the custard mix, stirring well. Return the custard to a clean pan and bring back to the boil, gently stirring continually. Remove from the heat, keep stirring, then pour the custard over the bananas and jam.

Sprinkle the top with desiccated coconut – this stops a skin from forming on the custard. Decorate with glacé cherries, leave to cool then refrigerate to set the custard.

A deli with
A DIFFERENCE

The ethos at The Little Deli Company in Hale is simple – to sell and produce fine local and continental food and drink at affordable prices

The Little Deli Company, set in the heart of Hale, began life in 2012 when two lifelong friends decided to pursue their passion for food and drink. David and Chris originally set up the business while maintaining their full-time jobs – and today, all their hard work and determination has paid off as they have watched their dream become a thriving reality.

When the business was born, it originally began life as a retail delicatessen. However the demand for sandwiches and salads using their heavenly array of local and continental meats, cheeses and other produce couldn't be ignored for long. The quality of the goodies quickly won over the Hale residents who have shared and supported The Little Deli Company's passion for shopping locally and supporting regional artisan producers from the start.

The Little Deli Company works with independent local farmers and producers, as well as specialist continental farmers and food importers. The aim is to provide everything under one roof, making their store a one-stop shop for food-lovers – you can pick up an authentic Spanish chorizo, locally produced craft beers, fine French saucisson and much more.

Today the deli acts as a foodie hub for Hale locals who drop in for a leisurely lunch or a coffee, cake and a chat. The inviting atmosphere combined with the friendly staff makes it a truly lovely place to while away a few hours. It boasts a delightful outdoor seating area – great on a sunny day, but you can always wrap one of their blankets around you if the Cheshire weather isn't quite as delightful as the food!

With enduring support from its regulars and plenty of new customers discovering its charms, The Little Deli Company has continued to grow from strength to strength. Two further sites have opened under David and Chris' brand 'The Elk' – a craft beer bar nearby in Hale and a restaurant and bar situated in Chorlton. David and Chris have plans for an expansion in 2016, too, which will see The Little Deli Company be in a position to offer even more to Hale's food-lovers.

The Little Deli Company
CHEESE & CHORIZO CROQUETTE BALLS

This is one of our personal favourite recipes as it incorporates cheese from three different countries and is unbelievably moreish. It makes a fantastic starter or small plate and is simple to prepare! Serves 4-6

Ingredients

100g diced cooking chorizo

100g Snowdonia Black Bomber cheddar cheese, grated

100g Lancashire crumbly cheese, grated

100g Gruyère, grated

2 grated apples

1 small white onion, finely chopped

50g chopped hazelnuts

A pinch of black pepper

10g finely sliced chives

20g cornflower, for rolling

1 egg, lightly beaten

Panko breadcrumbs, for coating

Olive oil, for sautéing

Vegetable oil, for deep-frying

Chilli-infused tomato coulis

Method

Lightly fry off the cooking chorizo in a pan with a little olive oil. In a separate bowl, mix the rest of the ingredients together, except for the cornflour, egg and panko breadcrumbs. Mould into 40g balls with your hands and add 1-2 cubes of the cooked chorizo into the centre of each.

Roll the balls into the cornflour. Dip the balls into the beaten egg and roll into the panko breadcrumbs. Deep fry in vegetable oil for 3-4 minutes until golden in colour with a crispy breadcrumb outer. Serve with a rocket salad and chilli-infused tomato coulis.

An Unforgettable EXPERIENCE

Set in a stunning rural location in the foothills of The Peak District, The Lord Clyde has struck the perfect balance of unpretentious fine dining in a beautiful country pub.

The Cheshire countryside is home to a pub with an astounding array of accolades to its name. However despite it being listed in the Michelin guide and having three AA rosettes, The Lord Clyde in Kerridge defines itself as a relaxing country pub serving unpretentious cuisine.

Ernst and Sarah took over the idyllic premises in September 2013, having been won over by the charm of the 19th-century stone-built weaver's cottages. They saw an opportunity to really do something different here – to bring fine dining into a warm and informal environment. Their success speaks for itself. The Lord Clyde is now listed in the Top 50 Gastro Pubs in the country, as well as in Harden's, The Good Food Guide and The Michelin Guide.

They welcome lots of new faces every month with people travelling from places as varied as Knutsford, Liverpool and even London to sample their dining experience. They also have many regulars who return week after week, which is something Sarah and Ernst are really proud of.

The location amidst the Cheshire countryside drives their culinary offerings, with local produce featuring heavily on the menu, which changes regularly to reflect the seasons. Ernst oversees the kitchen – having started working as a Chef at the age of 18, he has many years of experience under his belt, including staging at The Fat Duck, Restaurant Noma and Le Manoir aux Quat'Saisons.

The team at The Lord Clyde are passionate about every aspect of the pub experience, whether it's a quick pint in comfortable surroundings or a seasonal tasting menu: "Our dishes combine unpretentious modern British flavours with joyful creativity, fun and even a little surprise, all of which is complemented by our thoroughly cracking wine list. We also have a wonderful selection of beers and are proud to have Caske Marque accreditation for our real ales."

The Lord Clyde

The Lord Clyde

JAFFA CAKE

Serves 10

Ingredients

Bitter chocolate cream:

200g bitter chocolate, chopped

200g milk

200g double cream

4 egg yolks

Bitter chocolate brownie:

280g bitter chocolate

280g butter

400g sugar

6 eggs

130g plain flour

60g cocoa powder

Dehydrated bitter chocolate mousse:

150g bitter chocolate, chopped

3 egg yolks

150g egg white

50g sugar

Frozen orange aero:

150g orange purée

1 gelatine sheet, softened

55g egg yolks

10g sugar

150g double cream, semi-whipped

Orange gel:

300g orange juice

4g agar agar

20g sugar

To garnish:

Orange segments

Dried orange slices

Method

For the bitter chocolate cream

Cook the cream, sugar and egg yolks to 82°C to thicken and immediately pour over chopped chocolate. Leave for 1 minute, then stir and pour into a container to set.

For the bitter chocolate brownies

Preheat the oven to 180°C. Melt the chocolate and butter together over a bain marie. Beat the sugar and eggs until stiff. Sieve together the flour and cocoa powder. Fold the chocolate mixture into the egg mixture and then fold the dry mixture into the wet mixture. Pour into a lined tray and bake in the preheated oven until gooey; about 10–15 minutes.

For the dehydrated bitter chocolate mousse

Melt the chocolate and egg yolks together over a bain marie. Beat the egg whites and sugar until stiff and fold into the chocolate. Spread onto greaseproof paper and dehydrate at 60°C until dried and crispy.

For the frozen orange aero

Heat 50g of the orange purée in a pan and add gelatine sheet to dissolve. Whisk together the egg yolks and sugar. Pour the warmed orange purée mixture on to the egg mixture to cook slightly, then off the heat add the remaining 100g orange purée and let cool slightly before folding in the semi-whipped cream. Pour the mixture into an Isi whipper bottle and charge once with cartridge. Empty the mixture into external vacuum chamber, then vacuum, seal and freeze overnight.

For the orange gel

Bring all the ingredients to the boil for 2 minutes. Pour into a container to set, then blend until smooth to create a fluid gel.

To serve

Place 2 quenelles of the chocolate cream on the plate. Followed by pieces of the frozen orange aero.

Working quickly; arrange dots of the orange gel around; garnish with random shards of dried chocolate mousse, bitter chocolate brownie, dried orange slices and orange segments.

Perfect PRESERVES

Traditional farm-house recipes handed down through three generations, Mrs Darlington's Preserves have been made in Cheshire for over 35 years.

Mrs Darlington's Lemon Curd is nothing short of legendary in Cheshire. The Darlington family began making batches of their family recipe more than three decades ago in their farmhouse kitchen as a way of using up surplus eggs. Marion Darlington took her hand-crafted product to local retailers while on her egg delivery rounds and she was soon inundated with requests from customers who were won over by the unique taste of her zingy preserve.

With the help of the local brownies collecting jars for her and her two daughters putting the paper mop caps on the jars after school (paid the princely sum of halfpenny a jar!), Mrs Darlington began making about 100 jars of lemon curd each day. Soon, Mrs Darlington couldn't keep up with the ever-increasing demand in her kitchen, and Tom Darlington converted some of his farm buildings into a large kitchen so that production could be increased. Marion also took on her first member of staff, Janet, who would help to make the lemon curd as well as delicious cheesecakes, which they sold to local restaurants and pubs.

The range gradually expanded as the business grew – her mother's sweet apple chutney was one of the first additions, along with orange marmalade, lime curd and orange curd. Luckily a helpful Manchester-based pickles maker was on hand to sell Marion empty jars for her new products.

Today, the Mrs Darlington's range includes a whopping 80 products, but with both of Marion's daughters working in the business alongside their mother, it's safe to say that this is still a family business through and through. Sarah has been working alongside Marion for 27 years now, and in 2006 her sister Wendy was tempted to bring her marketing background to the business too. As the beautiful labels say, these gorgeous curds, jams, marmalades, pickles, chutneys, sauces and jellies truly are 'made with love'.

Mrs Darlingtons Preserves
LEMON AND LIME CHEESECAKE

We love this cheesecake recipe, as it is super simple and you can make it up to 24 hours ahead. It works equally well as a dinner party dessert or a weekend treat for the family – all our children give it a big thumbs up! Lemon curd is a great secret ingredient to pep up lots of desserts. If you enjoy the cheesecake, try adding a layer beneath the whipped cream of a pavlova or simply just swirl in a spoonful to some natural yoghurt and top with raspberries. It makes a great addition to ice cream, too! Serves 8

Ingredients

100g digestive biscuits

50g butter

1 tbsp caster sugar

250g tub mascarpone

375g can full-fat condensed milk

Juice of 1 lemon

Finely grated zest and juice of 2 limes

3 tbsp Mrs Darlington's Legendary Lemon Curd

Method

Crush the biscuits with a rolling pin until they're in fine crumbs. Melt the butter in a pan and then stir in the digestive crumbs and caster sugar until combined.

Use the back of a spoon to press the crumbs into the base of a 20cm (8 inch) shallow spring-form tin, then pop into the fridge to firm up whilst making the filling.

Put the mascarpone and condensed milk (make sure it's the full fat one or it won't set!), into a bowl and whisk with an electric hand whisk until smooth.

Add the lemon juice, lime juice and Mrs Darlington's legendary lemon curd plus nearly all the lime zest (keep a little back to garnish with) and whisk again until thick and creamy. Spoon on top of the biscuit base and level the top off using a small palette knife. Cover with cling film and chill for at least 2 hours. Decorate with the remaining lime zest.

Can You Keep A SECRET?

An exciting new dining concept is taking the Cheshire foodie scene by storm, thanks to the innovative pop-up restaurant My Secret Feasts. Welcome to a truly unique culinary experience...

Belinda and Rebecca, the faces behind the contemporary pop-up dining experience My Secret Feasts, are bringing bold flavours and an original way of eating and drinking to the people of Cheshire.

It all began at a festival in Oxfordshire, where Belinda and Rebecca were inspired by the long banquet tables where everyone dined together side by side with friends and strangers alike. With backgrounds in food and events, the foodie friends wanted to bring this joyful way of eating to their home county, and they certainly had the skills and drive to turn this dream into reality.

Their first pop-up dining event happened in Belinda's kitchen and it was a fabulous success. From here, they began looking for venues that could potentially play host to unique dinner parties. From churches to yurts and from an art gallery to a restored glass house, the ambitious duo are determined to find the most unusual venues to host their supper clubs – and so far, every venue they have approached has been really enthusiastic about being involved.

The concept is simple – a group of adventurous food-lovers book online to dine together at an undisclosed location to eat a secret menu. The only thing they know for sure? They are always in for a fun-filled evening of scrummy food and fabulous company.

The menu is dictated by the venue's facilities, but they are big fans of the fresh and vibrant flavours of Middle Eastern, North African and Turkish cuisines, so diners can expect to have their tastebuds awoken with herbs and spices and plenty of oomph. With eggs from their own hens, vegetables from their veggie patch and meat from local suppliers, freshness and flavour are paramount, right down to the homemade liqueurs that are used in the cocktails.

If dining with strangers isn't quite up your street, My Secret Feasts also host parties and corporate events. Hand over all responsibility to Belinda and Rebecca and relax and enjoy a magical atmosphere with your guests – let them whisk you all off to a secret location for an evening of conviviality.

With some form of entertainment always on hand to match the setting – think jazz singers, guitar players or even magicians – and a menu that has been designed to match the setting, it's safe to say that every single pop-up is a truly unique event.

My Secret Feasts
SPRING GREEN TERRINE

This terrine may be made from rather humble ingredients but when they all come together the result is really rather delicious. The sweet onion and garlic perfectly offset the saltiness of the bacon, whilst the creaminess of the egg brings a luxurious texture to the dish. It also looks great on the plate, especially if you use proper free-range eggs so that the yellow of the yolk jumps out of the dark green filling. Spring greens always sound so good but what can you actually do with them that is interesting? This terrine answers that question and, what is more, it is easy to make and inexpensive. Serves 10

Ingredients

400g smoked streaky bacon

8 tablespoons olive oil

2 onions, finely diced

500g spring greens, finely shredded

3 large cloves garlic, minced

6 large organic free-range eggs

50g homemade breadcrumbs

Salt and black pepper

Method

You will need a 1-litre loaf tin, lined with tin foil with plenty of extra hanging over the edge of the tin, so you can wrap up the terrine. Preheat the oven to 180°C.

Use 250-300g of the streaky bacon to line the base and sides of the foil-lined loaf tin, making sure that the bacon overhangs the edges so that you will be able to wrap it all the way around the terrine.

Chop the remaining bacon into small pieces and gently sauté the bacon pieces in the olive oil with the finely diced onions. Do not allow the onions to colour. After about 10 minutes, add the shredded spring greens and the minced garlic and continue to sauté, stirring from time to time, until everything has wilted down. Season with a little salt (not too much, as the bacon provides most of the saltiness) and plenty of freshly ground pepper.

Set aside to cool. Meanwhile boil 4 of the eggs for 5 minutes. Plunge the eggs into cold water and then peel them. In order that every serving gets a nice slice of yolk, trim the ends of the eggs to remove some excess white.

Now that the mixture is cooler, beat the remaining 2 eggs together and add to the mixture. Stir in the breadcrumbs and make sure that everything is combined thoroughly.

Fill the loaf tin with half the mixture and then line the eggs along the middle, making sure they are well nestled in. Finish off with the remaining mixture and press down well to ensure there are no gaps. Fold the bacon over so that everything is wrapped up and then use the excess foil to seal the terrine.

Set the loaf tin in a roasting tray and fill with boiling water until the level reaches two-thirds of the way up the loaf tin. Place in the preheated oven for 1 hour. Check the level of the water after 40 minutes, as it may need topping up.

Remove the terrine from the oven and gently lift out the foil package. Allow to cool completely before unwrapping the terrine. Slice into 10 reasonably thick pieces and serve with cornichons and crusty brown bread for a generous starter.

Now that's ORSOM

A unique blend of traditional cheese-making heritage with a modern approach to exciting new tastes and textures, Orsom Cheese has developed a range of handmade cheese with unique personalities.

The quirky British branding of Orsom Cheese captures the essence of these Cheshire-made cheeses perfectly – a subtle combination of traditional methods and exciting, modern flavours. Orsom Cheese was launched in April 2014 at the Chester Food and Drink Festival, where Cheshire foodies were immediately won over by the distinctive products.

However although the brand itself is new, the story behind the cheese begins back in 1957 when the Heler family first starting hand-making cheese on their dairy farm. Headed today by Mike Heler and his son George, the family business decided to create a range of speciality cheeses that would bring traditional hand-made products to the modern market.

The name, like all the best ideas, was developed around a table in the local pub, and it sums up exactly what they wanted the cheese to be. Something memorable amidst the plethora of cheeses available, something more than just nice, and something that would surprise people who thought they knew what traditional cheese tasted like. Something, well, Orsom.

With milk from the Heler dairy farm and the heritage of three generations of cheese-making, they had a good starting point. At Orsom, it's not just the cheeses that have won awards, their cows are award-winners too. The Orsom team are truly passionate about their pampered cows – from hoof manicures to mattresses for sleeping on, this herd of pedigree dairy cows, who graze on the lush pastures of the Cheshire plain, are at the heart of the business.

Each cheese in the four-strong range has its own character – in a flavour sense as well as in the unique packaging. Winston, for example – the strong, smooth and sophisticated Cheddar is encased in black wax and symbolised by the bowler hat, while Woodew, the cherry wood-smoked Cheddar is smoked naturally for 15 hours and portrayed with a classic smoking hat. Not ones to rest on their laurels however, the team are always being creative at the dairy looking for new characters to join the range.

It's fair to say that when it comes to character, these cheeses are simple yet flavourful, traditional yet modern, classic yet… totally Orsom.

Orsom Handmade Cheese

WINSTON CHEDDAR AND PARSNIP BREAD

A simple but incredibly tasty sharing bread that brings together the sweetness of the parsnip with the sweet, savoury and creamy notes of Winston Cheddar. Great to eat warm alongside a rich tomato or vegetable soup. Serves 4-6

Ingredients

1 tbsp cooking oil

1 large onion, chopped

100g Winston Cheddar cheese, grated

175g self-raising flour

½ tsp salt

1 tsp dried thyme

175g parsnip, peeled and grated

A pinch or a couple of grinds of black pepper

1 large egg, beaten

2-3 tbsp milk

Method

Preheat the oven to 180°C. Heat the oil in a large saucepan and cook the onion gently for 10 minutes, until soft and lightly coloured.

While this is cooking, mix together the grated Winston Cheddar, flour, salt, thyme, grated parsnip and black pepper in a mixing bowl.

While continuing to mix, add the cooked onion followed by the beaten egg and the milk, and mix to form a moist dough, adding a little extra milk if needed.

Take the dough out and kneed well to form a soft dough, then shape into a round.

Place the dough onto a lightly greased baking sheet and cook in the preheated oven for 45 minutes until golden.

Alpine CHIC

All the fun of the après ski without hitting the slopes first – Piste has brought the warm welcome of the Alps to the bustling high street of Tarporely.

James Hughes and his family have always shared a love of the Alps, delicious French food and the relaxed atmosphere of the famous après ski. When he decided to open his wine bar, it was this irresistible warmth and welcoming ambience he wanted to incorporate.

However Piste isn't just a venue for cosy winter evenings, the aim was very much for this to be a welcoming environment whatever the season. Thanks to James' sister Lucie's design skills, they have achieved just that – the décor is elegant and inviting, from the galleried staircases indoors to the tranquil Piste garden.

For James, family is at the heart of his business. Alongside Lucie, who manages marketing and graphics, his mum Val handles the accounts and, until recent ill-health, his brother-in-law Paul was head chef and business partner. Various other family members have worked in the kitchen and front of house, too – when needed it's all Hughes hands on deck!

Today the kitchen is led by former McLaren F1 team Head Chef Duncan Angus, whose experience cooking around the world has led to his incredible skills bringing flavours together. The menus are inspired by local seasonal produce, with stunning dishes for light lunches, relaxed evening meals, some truly special desserts, and sharing platters that are perfect for nibbling with a glass of wine.

Thanks to a commitment to fine local produce and attention to detail in the wine list, Piste has won numerous awards, including Marketing Cheshire's Restaurant of the Year in 2014 and 2015. James makes regular trips to Europe to meet independent wine producers, so customers can rely on having a choice of the very best wines that you won't find on other wine bar lists. They are also committed to having a varied range available by the glass – no excuse not to try a few!

The happy and energetic team are renowned for the warm welcome and attention to detail they give every customer, which is what has earned this wine bar a fond place in the hearts of the Tarporely residents. Whether you're enjoying the homemade breads and olives at the bar or tucking into the famous shin of beef, the customer service, excellent quality and value for money always leave customers with a little taste of Alpine hospitality.

Piste Wine Bar & Restaurant

Piste Wine Bar & Restaurant

SEVEN-HOUR BRAISED SHIN OF BEEF, HORSERADISH ROSTI, SHALLOT PURÉE, GLAZED SHALLOTS AND CONFIT VINE TOMATOES

This warming dish is a popular main course on our Mountain Menu. We use the very best quality beef for perfectly tender results. Serves 4

Ingredients

Beef Shin:

1kg boned shin of beef

1 onion, roughly chopped

1 bulb of garlic, chopped

1 carrot, diced

1 leek, diced

200ml water

100ml red cooking wine

1 litre good beef stock (save 200ml to roll)

Watercress, to garnish

Red wine jus, to serve

Horseradish Rosti:

2 potatoes, peeled

100g butter, melted

10g freshly grated horseradish

Salt and black pepper

A little olive oil

Shallot Purée:

100g shallots, peeled and diced

100ml vegetable stock

1 garlic clove

Salt and black pepper

100ml cream, to finish

Confit Tomato:

2 bunches of cherry tomatoes on the vine

Glazed shallots:

16 shallots

100ml red cooking wine

100ml Balsamic vinegar

1 bay leaf

Watercress, to garnish

Method

For the beef shin, preheat the oven to 150°C (Gas 2). Place the beef, onion, garlic, carrot, leek, water, wine and 800ml of the beef stock in an ovenproof dish and put in the oven. Leave to cook for 7 hours. Once cooked and tender, remove all the sinew, fat and gristle, leaving you with the shin. Season and add the remaining 200ml of beef stock. Mix thoroughly.

Lay two 30cm pieces of cling film on a chopping board. Place the picked and seasoned meat down the middle and roll into a tight sausage, tie a knot in one end and roll really tight. Place in the fridge and leave to cool for a few hours.

For the horseradish rosti, grate the potato then squeeze all of the water out into a tea towel. Place the potato in a bowl and add the melted butter, horseradish, salt and pepper and mix thoroughly. Warm a small blini pan with olive oil and a small amount of butter. Push one-quarter of the grated potato mixture into the blini pan, making sure mixture is pushed firmly into the pan.

Cook gently on a medium heat until the potato is a light golden brown. Turn the rosti over and cook on the other side. Once golden brown, remove from pan and allow to cool. Repeat to make 4 rostis altogether.

For the shallot purée, place all the ingredients in a pan apart from the cream and cook gently until soft. Use a blender and blitz into a smooth purée. Season and add enough cream to reach the right consistency.

For the confit tomato, cut each bunch of tomatoes into 4 and place on a roasting tray, season and add a little olive oil. Cook until soft, remove from oven and cool.

For the glazed shallots, blanch in boiling salted water. Peel once done. In a small pan reduce the wine and balsamic vinegar. Add the bay leaves and peeled shallots. Glaze in the reducing cooking liquor.

To build the dish, preheat the oven to 190°C (Gas 5). Cut the roll of shin into 4cm pieces. Seal in a hot sauté pan and place in the oven. Warm the shallot purée and, using a dessert spoon, make a swoosh across the plate. Place the hot rosti in the centre of the plate, top with the hot beef shin and decorate with 2 small bunches of the vine tomato and 4 glazed shallots. Pour 50ml of hot red wine jus onto the beef. Garnish with tiny sprigs of watercress and serve.

Spanish SIMPLICITY

The relaxed tapas and wine bar Porta has brought a taste of the Spanish way of life to Chester – nibbles, bar snacks, small plates, dinner… whatever you want to call it, there are no rules here.

When they opened their independent tapas bar Porta next door to their successful restaurant Joseph Benjamin, Joe and Ben knew exactly what they wanted to create. They wanted to capture the informal, relaxed vibes of Barcelona's tiny eateries, where people can sit for hours nibbling the finest cheeses, hams, breads and small plates while enjoying good wine and good company.

Informal and relaxed, no bookings are necessary, so diners can wander in and choose a bar stool or table to suit them. The only rule for Ben and Joe is that there are no rules – they want people to feel relaxed as soon as they walk in and to bring some Mediterranean vibes from the narrow cobbled streets of Barcelona to those of historic Chester.

Choose from a glass of wine or a bottle, choose a bar snack to accompany a beer, or a selection of cheese to go with a glass of wine, or choose a medley of dishes for a full meal – no pressure, no pretentions, no fuss. However that's not to say the food is simple to make. The Head Chef Javier (who hails from Madrid) works alongside Joe to create authentic homemade dishes from croquetas and patatas bravas to chorizo and lentil stew.

The brothers can be seen nipping back and forth between Porta and Joseph Benjamin next door – in fact you may even find them propping up the bar at Porta themselves when not working. They describe it as exactly the type of place they like to relax in – good food, good wine, good beer, good music.

The casual ambience has been welcomed by the Chester food-lovers, and its success sees it bustling throughout the week. So successful in fact that the brothers are planning a second venue in the near future, with rumours circulating around the Cheshire foodies that Altrincham might offer up the perfect location for it. We'll all have to wait patiently – Spanish-style – to find out…

Porta Tapas

SEARED PORK 'SECRETO IBERICO' WITH MOJO VERDE

This dish is a bit of a speciality. 'Secreto Iberico' is the name of this cut of pork sourced from the shoulder of acorn-fed Iberian pigs. The meat is highly marbled and, contrary to our domestic cultural instincts, is best served pink. This is only possible when using meat of the highest quality and should not be done with other cuts. The sauce 'mojo verde' originates in the Canary Islands and is great with grilled meats and fish. In place of the Secreto, you could use any other cut of pork with similarly delicious results. Serves 6

Ingredients

1kg Secreto Iberico

1 tbsp sweet smoked paprika

1 tsp fennel seeds

Small handful of thyme

3 cloves garlic, roughly chopped

A splash of olive oil

Mojo verde:

2 green peppers, roughly chopped

100g large green chillies, deseeded and roughly chopped

2 cloves garlic, chopped

1 bunch coriander, including stalks, roughly chopped

1½ tsp ground cumin

1½ tsp dried oregano

1½ tbsp white wine vinegar

1 tbsp caster sugar

6 tbsp olive oil

Method

Marinate the Secreto Iberico in the paprika, fennel seeds, thyme, garlic and olive oil.

To make the mojo verde, whizz the peppers, chillies, garlic, coriander, cumin and oregano in a food processor until fine. Add the vinegar, sugar and oil.

To serve, fry the Secreto Iberico in a hot pan, until browned but still pink, approximately 2 minutes on each side. Rest for 5 minutes. Slice neatly. Fan out the pork on the plate. Put a spoonful of the mojo verde on top. Lightly dust with some smoked paprika, small pinch Maldon salt and a drizzle of olive oil.

PURPLE SPROUTING BROCCOLI WITH ROMESCO SAUCE

One of our new favourite tapas dishes. Ben and I have been addicted to broccoli in various recipes all winter. The trick to this one is letting the broccoli sit still in the pan and get a little charred and burnt around the edges. Romesco sauce is a Catalan speciality of almonds and red peppers. It also goes brilliantly with fish. Serves 4

Ingredients

400g purple sprouting broccoli, trimmed

35ml olive oil

40g ciabatta bread, ripped into small pieces

40g flaked almonds, plus extra to garnish

2 garlic cloves, chopped

½ tsp chilli flakes

½ tsp ground cumin

1 tsp sweet smoked paprika

1 tbsp ketchup

1 tbsp Sherry vinegar

400g tin chopped tomatoes

180g piquillo peppers

Salt and pepper

Method

First make the Romesco sauce. Heat the olive oil in a large frying pan/skillet. Add the ciabatta and almonds and fry until golden. Lower the heat. Add the garlic, chilli, cumin and paprika, fry gently for 1 minute. Tip into a saucepan along with the ketchup, vinegar, tomatoes and piquillo peppers.

Bring to the boil, simmer for 30 minutes. Tip into a blender, purée until as smooth as you like it, and add salt and pepper. Set aside. Serve the sauce at room temperature or slightly warm.

Stir-fry the broccoli until tender and slightly charred. Add a little salt and pepper. Place a spoonful of Romesco on the plate, pile some broccoli on top and sprinkle a few extra flaked almonds on top to garnish.

A home FROM HOME

Once the Lord Mayor's 'residence', the elegant Regency building in the historic centre of Nantwich is now home to Residence Restaurant & Bar – the perfect venue for wining, dining or sipping cocktails.

For owner Ben Rafferty, the success of his Nantwich gem, Residence Restaurant & Bar, is the culmination of many years in the hospitality industry. From his early days as a pot washer, through many exciting years as a bartender around the world to various management roles, it's fair to say he knows a thing or two about the eating and drinking industry. When the opportunity came up to open a restaurant in the stunning Georgian mansion house in 2007 – how could he refuse?

As its plethora of awards testifies, Residence offers something special to the Nantwich dining scene. The cocktail bar offers a relaxed atmosphere through the week, buzzing at the weekends, with dazzling drinks being shaken and stirred by knowledgeable bartenders – choose from the impressive menu and they will whip it up just the way you like it. Everything is fresh, from the homemade cordials to the freshly squeezed limes.

Freshness and quality are key when it comes to the food, too. Trusted local suppliers ensure seasonal produce is delivered daily, and everything is made in-house, from the irresistible bread to the beautiful pastries that adorn the afternoon tea stands. Whether you're having a fixed price lunch menu or treating yourself to a rare-breed steak, the talented chefs deliver excellent quality.

Special nights are always in the calendar, from BYO nights to surf and turf nights – keep your eye on the website for up-to-date details.

With a sunny terrace outside for summer al fresco meals, private dining options and a large function suite, Residence Restaurant & Bar caters for a wide variety of occasions. It's a popular wedding venue – and even holds a licence for civil ceremonies – thanks to its charismatic style and elegant décor. What sets it apart is the intimacy, exclusive hire options, as well as the freedom to plan your special day exactly as you want it.

Free of charge Sunday venue hire is the ideal choice for Christenings and birthdays – it's best to give them a call to discuss the details, but with a dedicated Events Coordinator on hand, it's easy to plan the perfect party.

Residence Bar & Restaurant

BABA GHANOUSH, KING SCALLOPS AND IBÉRICO CHORIZO

King scallops have always been a great-selling dish and have never been off the menu since opening. We vary the menu 4 to 6 times a year and this dish has been a really popular version! Serves 1

Ingredients

3 king scallops

1 aubergine

1 garlic clove, sliced into spears

1 tsp cumin or curry powder

A small bunch of fresh coriander

3 slices Ibérico chorizo

A little olive oil

A little butter

Salt and black pepper

Chilli oil, for drizzling

Pea shoots, to garnish

Method

Preheat the oven to 200°C.

Wash, prepare and trim the king scallops, then score criss crosses on the top of each.

Take the aubergine, score it and prick with the garlic, rub with olive oil and the cumin or curry powder and wrap in foil. Cook for 20 minutes until soft in the centre. Scoop out the centre flesh. Blend with the coriander and season with salt and pepper.

Pan-fry the king scallops on a high heat with a little oil for 1 minute on each side, then finish with a little butter and spoon over to coat.

Pan-fry the slices of Ibérico chorizo for 1 minute, pressing them down in the pan to retain their shape.

Place a spoon full of the baba ghanoush under each scallop, drizzle some chilli oil over and garnish with pea shoots.

PORNSTAR MARTINI

Ingredients

Serve in a chilled coupette glass plus 50ml shot glass of Prosecco

30ml vanilla vodka

15ml Passoa liqueur

50ml pineapple juice

5ml squeezed lemon

½ squeezed passion fruit

To garnish

5mg sugar, flamed

½ passion fruit

Method

Add all the cocktail ingredients to a glass with some ice and muddle for 15 seconds.

Strain through a hawthorn strainer and also through a small sieve.

Garnish with flamed sugar and passion fruit.

The Essence of
ITALIAN LIFE

A celebration of five generations of family life and business, Rolando's brings a taste of the Italian life to Lymm.

"Enjoying a meal with family and friends is the main ingredient for any Italian dish." This is the motto for the family-run Rolando's eatery in the heart of Lymm. It aims to bring the warm and welcoming environment of the village piazza to Cheshire, giving food lovers a taste of the real Italian life.

Rolando's family originate from a tiny village called Picinisco, where simple dishes were made from the garden's bounty, local olive oil and fresh handmade pasta. Grandfather Domenico, a carpenter, came to Manchester in 1895 and began a successful business crafting barrel pianos. With a thriving family of six children, he began selling Italian food and wine too, which became the focus of the family business once the piano industry declined in the 1920s.

Today the dishes at Rolando's are based on the life that the family cherishes from their Italian heritage: fresh ingredients that are simple but of outstanding quality. The pizza stone in the open kiln oven ensures their amazing artisan pizzas are famous throughout Lymm and beyond. Everything is freshly made the way it has been for generations, from the classic pasta to the pizza dough, not to mention the famous gelato.

The deliciously silky smooth gelato is gaining a formidable reputation in the area and is enjoyed in cones, sundaes or waffles. Vibrant and fruity or rich and chocolatey, the freshly made gelato can transport you to the Italian piazza in an instant. The gelato is all made on the premises and offers a kaleidoscope of flavours, with new recipes being developed all the time, much to the delight of their many growing gelato fans.

Pizza and pasta are available all the time, as well as sandwiches, soups and salads in the day time, which includes the option to create your own sandwich on a home-baked ciabatta. Simply select the meat, cheese, salad and dressing you would like and the staff will do the rest – think bresaola, salami, Parma ham, mortadella, gorgonzola or provolone. With a select wine list to choose from and a special children's menu too, nothing is overlooked at this popular Italian gem.

Rolando's

Rolando's
CALZONE

A traditional folded pizza with a delicious dipping sauce for the crust. If you have a pizza stone you can use this and adjust the cooking time down appropriately. Serves 1

Ingredients

Calzone:

1 dough ball, about 220g

150g pizza mozzarella, cubes or ribbons

60g ragù sauce

30g sliced pepperoni

100g cooked pollo piccante (see below)

40g mushrooms, sliced

Marinated garlic oil, for brushing

40g tomato pulpa

Peperonata sauce, for serving on the side (see below)

Pollo piccante:

1 small chicken breast

3 tbsp olive oil

½ tsp chilli powder

A pinch of salt

Peperonata sauce:

2 tbsp extra virgin olive oil

1 clove garlic, peeled and pressed

½ large onion, peeled and finely sliced

500g red peppers, sliced into strips

225g peeled plum tomatoes (or fresh when in season, chopped)

Salt and pepper, to taste

Chopped fresh basil and parsley

Method

To make the pollo piccante, chop the chicken breast, heat the olive oil in a large pan, add the chicken and fry for about 5 minutes. Then add the chilli powder, salt and finish frying until cooked through.

To make the peperonata sauce, heat the oil in a large pan, fry the garlic and onion. Add the peppers and cook for about 10 minutes over medium heat. Pour in the tomatoes, stir and simmer for another 20 minutes on low heat. Add salt and pepper. Sprinkle with basil and parsley and let it cool. Place the mixture in a blender and chop until becomes creamy.

Preheat the oven to 240°C.

For the calzone, spread the dough ball into a circle approx 12 inches. Put the cheese into the centre of the circle, add the ragù, chicken, mushrooms and finally pepperoni. Fold the dough over into a semi-circle and push the edges to seal. This is important to keep from leaking.

Trim the surplus with a pizza wheel and pull into shape.

Bake in the preheated home oven on a baking tray for 10-12 minutes. The calzone should be brown on top when cooked, like a loaf of bread.

Take out of the oven and brush with marinated garlic oil and top with warm tomato pulpa. Serve with the peperonata sauce for dipping on the side.

Scandinavian STYLE

A passion for Scandinavian food, design and living led Debbie Quinn to open her dream bar and restaurant The Salt Bar in the summer of 2013 on the historic cobbled streets of Macclesfield.

Debbie Quinn is something of a community champion in Macclesfield. Passionate about bringing local people together, celebrating food and promoting the town's community spirit, her culinary journey began long before she opened her famous restaurant The Salt Bar in the centre of town.

After volunteering at the local Barnaby Festival, Debbie wanted to become more involved in the community and decided to organise a farmer's market. It was so successful, she set about organising a new market alongside her friend Jane Munro – Treacle Market was born with an initial 40 stalls. Today it is so popular it boasts over 150 stalls of food, drink, arts, crafts and antiques, and is a thriving and bustling hub for the Macclesfield community on the last Sunday of every month.

Such commitment to community hasn't been overlooked and in January 2016 Debbie and Jane were named in the Queen's New Year's Honour's List to be awarded the British Empire Medal (BEM) for services to business and the community for The Treacle Market.

With new-found confidence, it was in the summer of 2013 when Debbie took the plunge and opened the doors of her own restaurant and bar, The Salt Bar. A fan of Scandinavian design and food, Debbie had been won over by the lifestyle on trips to Copenhagen and Stockholm. The Salt Bar, which featured in BBC2's The Restaurant Man, is small and cosy with just 34 covers. The simplicity of the design and the warmth of the welcome can transport you to Scandinavia in an instant.

Debbie is heavily involved in planning the menus. She aims to keep it simple with a focus on using the best quality ingredients. They smoke their own food in-house, such as fish, duck and nuts, and they do their own pickling on-site, too. Traditional Scandinavian classics make up most of the menu, but there are plenty of modern twists too.

Upstairs, The Salt Rooms offer three boutique bedrooms, which are the embodiment of style and comfort – and, of course, include a delicious home-cooked breakfast as well.

The Salt Bar

PICKLED SALMON (INKOKT LAX)

If you've not tried pickled fish before, this is a great way to try it. A light sweet
pickle, this salmon makes a delicious starter. Serves 4

Ingredients

250-300g salmon fillet

Salt

1 small red onion

2 medium carrots

2 tbsp allspice berries

200ml water

200ml distilled vinegar

200g sugar

Method

Cover the fish in salt and leave to cure for 2 hours. Rinse thoroughly, dry and cut into
1 inch cubes.

Bring the water, vinegar and sugar to the boil, add the onion, allspice berries and carrot
and simmer for five minutes. Cool to a temperature of 60°C and pour over the salmon.

Chill preferably overnight, but after 3-4 hours the fish should be firm and ready to eat.
Serve with Knackerbröd (Scandinavian crispbread).

The Salt Bar

VENISON WITH LIQUORICE SAUCE SERVED WITH POTATO TERRINE (RÅDJURSFILÉ MED LAKRITSSÅS)

Salty liquorice is an ingredient that is very typically Scandinavian. It marries perfectly with venison in this recipe and has always proved to be extremely popular with customers when it appears on our menu. Serves 4

Ingredients

4 venison steaks

Salt and pepper

Olive oil, for frying

Potato Terrine:

50g butter

4 whole cloves garlic, lightly crushed

300ml double cream

150ml whole milk

A few sprigs of fresh thyme

4 floury potatoes, such as Maris Piper

Salt and pepper

Liquorice Sauce:

60g Turkish Peber salted liquorice sweets

12.5ml red wine

12.5ml beef stock

1 tsp balsamic vinegar

2 tsp brown sugar

1 tsp butter

Method

For the potato terrine, preheat the oven to 210°C. Melt the butter in a saucepan and add the whole crushed garlic (including the skins). Gently fry for 2-3 minutes. Add the thyme, cream and milk. Bring almost to the boil, reduce the heat and simmer for around 20 minutes.

Once it has reduced to a thick cream, sieve and discard the thyme and garlic.

Peel and wash the potatoes. Slice thinly into the cream mixture, preferably using a mandoline. Mix well, allowing the potatoes to soak up the mixture.

Line a deep roasting tin with greaseproof paper. Layer the potatoes and then pour over the remaining mix. Cover with more greaseproof paper and place another roasting tin on top to keep the terrine compact. Cook in the preheated oven for 2 hours.

The venison steaks are best served rare. Remove the steaks from the fridge and bring to room temperature.

For the liquorice sauce

Place all the sauce ingredients in a pan and bring to the boil. Simmer for 10 minutes until reduced to a thick sauce, whisking frequently.

Rub the steaks with a little olive oil and season with salt and pepper. Heat a non-stick frying pan until very hot, fry the steaks for 2 minutes on each side. Allow to rest before serving.

All Hale The
DEEP SOUTH

Craft beers, bourbon, cocktails, slow-smoked meats, lobster, steak, hot dogs and burgers – a taste of the American deep south has arrived in the centre of Hale. Welcome to Stockyard.

When the meat smoker has been imported specially from the States, you know the restaurant owner means business. You know this isn't just going to be a run of the mill burger joint with a nod to the USA. For Dominic Clancy, bringing authentic southern BBQ cuisine to leafy Hale meant getting the meat and the liquor just right – and it's fair to say he's achieved just that.

Owned by Manchester Beers Limited, Stockyard has a craft beer selection unlike anything else in the area. The bar offers ten draught beers, from Samuel Adams Boston Lager to Manchester's famous Boddingtons. The fridges contain a plethora of bottled beers to try, too.

The cocktail menu is ever-changing and there are always intriguing specials as well as tried-and-tested classics. Of course it wouldn't be an American bar without a staggering whiskey menu – it will take quite a few visits to try all of the bourbon and rye on offer here.

Now, on to the food. Smoked bourbon sticky chicken wings, loaded nachos, jumbo shrimp cocktail, chilli cheese skins… and that's just for starters. The burger menu reads like a meaty tribute to American culture – try a Plain Jane, The Johnny Cash, Philly Steak, Tony the Greek or Los Pollos. Hot dogs, steaks, lobster, salads and sharing platters are all on offer, too.

With the lobsters imported from the icy Atlantic shore of Canada and the meat sourced from the renowned Mettrick's butchers, Head Chef, Phil Piskor, can tell you the provenance of every cut he uses in the restaurant. When you've gone to the effort of buying the very best smoker from the States, you're not going to waste it with anything other than the finest meats. The St Louis ribs are smoked for 6 hours and the famous house-smoked pulled pork gets its incredible flavour from a 16-hour smoking period. Served with cornbread and house slaw on the side, this is the ultimate melt-in-the-mouth deliciousness.

The Stockyard
ROLLERCOLA RIBS

We part-smoke our ribs in our in-house American smoker. We have listed an alternative method for you at home, so you don't miss out on the amazing smokey taste. Serves 2

Ingredients

2 racks of baby pork ribs (ask your butcher to remove the membrane from the back of the ribs)

2-litre bottle of regular (full-fat) cola of your choice

1 star anise

½ tsp fennel seeds

15ml liquid smoke (available online and good cookshops)

Thin fries, to serve

2 portions Cajun Slaw (see Smokey Mountain recipe or use store-bought), to serve

Rib Rub:

¼ cup sweet paprika

4½ tsp freshly ground black pepper

4½ tsp dark brown sugar

1 tbsp salt

1½ tsp celery salt

1½ tsp cayenne pepper

1½ tsp garlic powder

1½ tsp dry mustard

1½ tsp ground cumin

Method

Preheat the oven to 170°C.

Combine all the rib rub ingredients together. Apply the rib rub generously to the baby back ribs, ensuring it is well massaged into the meat, for best results try to do this 24 hours prior to cooking.

Lay the ribs flat on an oven try and add the cola, enough to just cover the ribs, plus the star anise, fennel seeds and liquid smoke.

Completely cover the tray with foil and pinch around well to make a good seal. Place into the preheated oven for 1 hour 30 minutes.

Once out of the oven, carefully lift the ribs out of the tray and place onto a new, greaseproof-lined oven tray. You will be left with a tray full of juices/cooking liquor from the ribs. Carefully pour half of the remaining juices through a sieve and into a saucepan, and skim off any fat.

On a high heat, reduce the liquor/cooking juices until it becomes a syrup resembling thin honey. Brush this liberally back over the ribs and put them back in the oven for another 5-10 minutes until sticky and glazed.

Serve with Cajun slaw and fries.

The Stockyard
SMOKEY MOUNTAIN

This recipe has been adapted to suit home cooks. In our restaurant the pork is smoked in our industrial smoker, however you can easily replicate this smokey flavour by using 'liquid smoke'. This can be bought from supermarkets or online. Serves 2

Ingredients

4 x good-quality 80/20 unseasoned chuck steak burger patties

2 slices beef tomato

2 leaves of cos lettuce, finely sliced

½ red onion, finely sliced

1 dill pickle, finely sliced

4 slices American-style burger cheese

2 wooden skewers

Brioche Buns:

125ml warm water

1 tsp dried yeast

1.5 tbsp warm milk

1 tbsp golden caster sugar

225g strong flour, plus extra for dusting

½ tsp salt

2 tbsp unsalted butter, softened

1 large egg, plus 1 beaten egg, for glazing

Pulled Pork:

½ onion, sliced

1 bay leaf

¼ tbsp mustard powder

¼ tbsp smoked paprika

1 tsp ground black pepper

A good pinch of salt

500g pork shoulder, boned with rind attached and tied (ask your butcher to do this)

5ml liquid smoke (hickory)

1 bottle of your favourite bbq sauce

Cajun Slaw:

1 carrot, peeled and grated

1/6 white cabbage, very finely sliced

1/6 red cabbage, very finely sliced, washed and well drained (otherwise you will have purple slaw!)

3 drops Tabasco sauce

A pinch of Cajun seasoning (or more if you like it hot!)

25ml mayo or to taste

2ml white wine vinegar or to taste

Method

Brioche Buns:

Mix the water, yeast, milk and sugar in a bowl. Stand for 5 minutes until frothy. Tip the flour and salt into a large mixing bowl, add the butter and rub together with your fingertips until the mixture resembles breadcrumbs. Make a well in the centre of the buttery flour and add the yeast mixture and the egg. Use your hands to mix it into a sticky dough – if the mixture feels too wet at this stage, it will come together when kneading. Tip the dough out onto a floured work surface. Knead the dough for 10 minutes. It will still be very sticky but don't be tempted to add too much flour. The dough is ready when soft and bouncy. Place in an oiled bowl, cover with cling film and set aside to rise for 1-3 hours or until doubled in size.

Once doubled in size, knock the air out and knead for 2 minutes. It won't be as sticky, but add flour if needed. Divide the dough evenly in two. Roll into balls and arrange on a lined baking tray. Loosely cover with oiled cling film and leave for about 1 hour or until doubled in size again. Meanwhile, preheat the oven to 200°C (180°C fan, gas 6) and place a baking tray at the bottom.

Uncover and brush the buns with egg glaze. Pour a cup of water into the baking tray at the bottom of the oven to create steam. Place the bun tray on a shelf above. Bake for 20 minutes or until golden, then leave to cool on a wire rack.

Pulled Pork:

Preheat the oven to 160°C (140°C fan, gas 3). Scatter the onions and bay leaf in the bottom of a large roasting tin. Mix the mustard powder, paprika, black pepper with a good pinch of salt. Rub this all over the pork, making sure you rub it into all the crevices. Place the pork, rind-side up, on top of the onions. Pour 200ml water and the liquid smoke into the bottom of the tin, wrap well with foil and bake for 2 hours 30 minutes to 3 hours or until you can easily pull it apart.

Lift the pork onto a large plate or tray. Remove the string and peel off the skin. Using 2 forks, shred the meat into chunky pieces. Add 3-4 tbsp (or to your taste!) of the barbecue sauce to the meat and toss everything well to coat This can be done up to 2 days ahead – simply cover the tray in foil and chill until ready to use.

Cajun Slaw:

In a bowl combine all the ingredients together, cover and refrigerate until needed.

Making your Smokey Mountain:

Get a griddle or frying pan on a medium heat ready for the burgers and season the patties with a little salt. Place the burgers into the pan for 1½-2 minutes each side, depending on how pink you like them (more if you like them well done). While the burgers are cooking start to assemble your buns. Toast under the grill before adding a little bbq sauce to the inside of the top bun, followed by the sliced tomato. On the bottom bun place the lettuce, red onion, dill pickle and a mound of slaw. Once you have turned your burgers add the cheese to the top whilst you allow the other side to cook. Get your pulled pork at the ready (if it's been made in advance add a little bbq sauce to it and microwave until hot). Place two burgers on each of the pre-assembled buns then mound the pulled pork on top. Put the top of the bun on ensuring the tomato doesn't slide off and secure with a wooden skewer. Enjoy!

Passion for PUGLIA

Sugo Pasta Kitchen in Altrincham is the only place to experience authentic southern Italian cooking in Manchester and Cheshire.

Anyone who has visited southern Italy can tell you that there is something special about the pasta served there – and for Sugo Pasta Kitchen part-owners and chefs, Jonny Marcogliese and Alex De Martiis, it was a passion they wanted to share.

Being half-Italian and half-English, and both of their families being from the Puglia region of Italy, the pair of foodies soon began discussing how difficult it was to get an amazing bowl of pasta the way their Nonnas made it.

"Pasta restaurants tend to tailor their dishes to British tastes," explains Alex, "but today people travel much more and are adventurous when it comes to trying authentic produce and regional dishes". Spotting this gap in the market and confident that the Altrincham locals would embrace the bold flavours of southern Italy, Sugo Pasta Kitchen opened in the summer of 2015.

Wooden sharing tables, an open kitchen, a passionate team and a daily-changing blackboard menu is what you can expect to find at Sugo Pasta Kitchen.

Vibrant chilli, zesty lemon, fresh parsley, rich San Marzano tomatoes – the dishes pack a punch when it comes to taste. Ingredients are either sourced locally (the meat and vegetables, for example) or selected from the finest suppliers in Italy to ensure that every ingredient is the best possible. Dried pasta, which is favoured in many southern Italian dishes, is imported from Puglia, and even the beautiful crockery was bought in the region.

The open kitchen means that everything happens in front of the diners. Nothing is hidden and no short-cuts are taken – if a dish needs to simmer for 8 hours, then it will be simmered for 8 hours. Sugo Pasta Kitchen really is a one-off and is now setting the standard for Italian food in Manchester and Cheshire. With only 24 covers, make sure you book in advance!

ABOUT SUGO...

WE'RE HERE TO SHARE WITH YOU OUR PASSION
FOR REAL SOUTHERN ITALIAN COOKING.
WHETHER IT'S OUR ORECCHIETTE THAT COMES TO US
FROM PUGLIA OR OUR HOMEMADE SOTT'OLIO WHICH
WE LEARNT FROM OUR NONNA'S: OUR AIM IS TO
GIVE YOU OUR HERITAGE ON A PLATE!

JUST SO YOU KNOW.....
WE DON'T PRE-COOK OUR PASTA EVERYTHING IS COOKED TO ORDER
SOUTHERN ITALIANS EAT PASTA AL DENTE!
WE SOURCE THE BEST PRODUCE WE CAN, LOCALLY OR DIRECT FROM
SOUTHERN ITALY. YOUR PLATES HAVE BEEN HAND MADE IN PUGLIA!
TUTTI A TAVOLA E BUON APPETITO! X

SUGO
PASTA KITCHEN

Sugo Pasta Kitchen

CALAMARATA ALLO SCOGLIO CON ZENZERO

We've chosen this dish partly because we love it, but also because we feel that it highlights one of our main aims at Sugo. Pasta allo scoglio is badly represented in restaurants around the country, due to varying factors (bad ingredients, wrong methods/timing, lack of passion) and we hope that we go some way to putting this right. The addition of ginger gives the dish a real lift and subtly illustrates how we like to experiment with ingredients. More than any of that, of course, we've added the dish because we love to eat it! Serves 2

Ingredients

200g bronze drawn Calamarata di Gragnano pasta

2 large glugs of Italian extra virgin olive oil

8 raw shell on tiger prawns

3 garlic cloves, minced

A thumb-size piece of ginger, finely chopped

1 whole red chilli, finely sliced with seeds

2 whole baby squid with tentacles, cleaned and cut into rings

2 handfuls of fresh mussels, cleaned and de-bearded

2 handfuls of fresh baby plum San Marzano tomatoes, halved

1 glass of Italian dry white wine

Juice of half a lemon

A handful of fresh parsley, finely chopped

Maldon sea salt

Method

Bring a large pan of water to the boil, season generously (until it tastes like the sea), add the Calamarata pasta and cook until al-dente.

Meanwhile, in a large, heavy-based non-stick frying pan, heat the olive oil on a medium heat. Add the prawns, lightly sear, and season with a pinch of Maldon sea salt. Add the garlic, ginger and chilli and fry for a few minutes to infuse. Add the baby squid and the mussels, turn the heat up and fry until the squid takes on colouration.

At this point add the baby San Marzano tomatoes (squashing them in your hand as you place them in the pan), a pinch of Maldon sea salt and the wine to de-glaze the pan. Once the wine has reduced slightly, put the lid on the pan and reduce the heat (this process will help marry the wine, San Marzano tomatoes and fish liquor). Cook until the mussels have opened, the baby squid is tender and the prawns have cooked through (this will take about 5 minutes).

Once the pasta has cooked until al-dente, drain it (not heavily as you want the pasta to retain some of its cooking water to help with the finish) and add it to the pan with the fish. Turn the heat up, mix well and allow the liquor to reduce while amalgamating with the Calamarata. Once the pasta has soaked up the majority of the liquor, squeeze in the lemon juice and allow it to cook out for a further minute. Finish by tossing the chopped parsley through the pan and serve immediately.

a MILLER'S TALE

Walk Mill is set in the Cheshire countryside, only a short drive nearby from Chester. A water mill with a fascinating history with beautiful local walks and an enticing café and shop selling flour, cakes and loaves – this Cheshire gem has plenty to explore.

When the Jones family uncovered the remains of a 13th-century mill on their family-run arable farm, they set about the daunting task of bringing it back to life. After much hard work, Ben Jones and his family rebuilt the mill on the ancient foundations and have now been producing stone-ground flour there for over 7 years.

The area is a perfect spot for a stroll around the Cheshire countryside, with centuries-old footpaths criss-crossing the farmland. Despite the mill being at the heart of this walker's paradise, the name Walk Mill actually came from its original history as a fuller's mill (cloth mill) and the 'walkers' whose job it was to clean the cloth.

This is just part of the intriguing history discovered by the Jones family as they pieced together the story of their mill. The original floor tiles have been given a new lease of life in the Miller's Kitchen and mill area and hand-made bricks that were excavated can be seen surrounding the fireplace. The original sack hoist and damsel have also been put back to use in the mill today.

All this attention to tradition and heritage doesn't stop with the building's structure, of course. The stone-ground flour is all made from an English wheat variety grown in the fields surrounding the mill (no food miles!), which is slowly stone-ground from whole grains to preserve all the nutrients.

The different grades on offer – wholemeal, white and malted – are created by various levels of sifting. No bleaching is involved and each grade makes fantastic cakes, bread and pastry. Just pop into our café, The Miller's Kitchen, to taste the products with a cup of tea!

Freshly made goodies are on offer every day in this popular on-site café, from sandwiches, toasties and soups to flapjack, scones and cakes. Of course whole loaves are available to buy, too, along with the flour itself so that you can whip up tasty treats in your own kitchen. The flour is already been used by renowned restaurants across Cheshire, and is available at many of our county's retailers and farm shops, too.

Walk Mill
WHOLEMEAL SCONES

Using our Walk Mill Stone-ground Wholemeal Flour gives the scones a nice texture and earthy flavour due to the bran. People are always surprised about how light our wholemeal scones are, and this is due to the addition of natural yoghurt, which has, until this book, been kept under wraps as our secret ingredient! Serves 9

Ingredients

450g Walk Mill Stone-ground Wholemeal Flour

125g butter

1 tbsp caster sugar

2 tsp baking powder

½ tsp salt

1 egg

50g sultanas

1 tbsp golden syrup

250g natural yoghurt

Method

Preheat the oven to 220°C.

Put the flour, butter, sugar, baking powder and salt into a mixing bowl and rub the butter in until the mixture is the consistency of breadcrumbs.

Add the egg, sultanas, golden syrup and yoghurt, and mix again until a wet dough is formed.

Turn out onto a flour-dusted work surface. Flatten out to about 2cm in depth then cut out about 9 scones with a fluted scone cutter. Place the scones on a baking tray lined with baking parchment.

Bake in the preheated oven for approximately 15-20 minutes until the scones are golden brown and 'bounce' back if pressed down.

Escape to the
COUNTRY

Willington Hall is a small privately-owned hotel with a big reputation for its beautiful setting, excellent customer service and epicurean British country cooking.

Willington Hall might just be one of Cheshire's best-kept secrets. The twelve-bedroom country house in idyllic countryside was built in 1829 by the great grandfather of the former owner of the hotel, Mr Richard Tomkinson, whose portrait features in the dining room. The Begbie family began a new phase in its splendid history when they took over the reins in 1999 and restored it to the stunning venue it is today.

Head Chef Paul-Anthony fell in love with the charms of Willington Hall the first time he saw it and it's easy to see why – the characterful building sits within immaculately sculpted gardens with rural views extending over the beautiful Cheshire countryside around.

For Paul-Anthony, the setting influences every aspect of his cooking. His aim is to encapsulate the traditional British country feel of the 19th century house with classic dishes and the finest seasonal ingredients, but give them exciting twists using 21st century cooking techniques and creative culinary flair. Paul-Anthony looks forward to each ingredient coming into season and planning his menus around them – whether it's meat from neighbouring organic farms, seasonal fruits and vegetables from local suppliers or herbs from the on-site kitchen garden.

The Gainsborough Restaurant is the jewel in the crown, offering fine dining options for lunch and dinner, as well as its famous Sunday lunches. It has become renowned in the local area and welcomes return visitors who have been won over by the attention to detail in the food, service and ambience. For lighter bites, the Drawing Room Bar is the place to go – it is also an ideal setting to enjoy a traditional afternoon tea. In winter the Study Bar offers a sumptuous environment for a fine whisky and in summer the Terrace is a popular spot for a glass of Champagne.

Well known for hosting private functions and weddings, the team at Willington Hall have earned a reputation for making every event incredibly special – it's all down to attention to detail and going above and beyond to give every occasion the personal touch. Each bedroom is furnished to the luxurious standards in keeping with the elegant Edwardian country style.

Willington Hall aims to offer something for everyone. Whether it's a stroll around the gardens and a coffee, a cup of tea and a freshly baked scone, a full Champagne afternoon tea, a light lunch or a gourmet dinner, every guest will be treated to a warm Cheshire welcome and personal customer service.

Photo courtesy of SMH photography

Photo courtesy of Victoria Photographic

Photo courtesy of SMH photography

Photo courtesy of Victoria Photographic

Photo courtesy of Victoria Photographic

Willington Hall

PIGEON AND BLACK PUDDING SAUSAGE ROLL WITH PIGEON, BEET SALAD AND KALE PESTO DRESSING

We cook seasonal British country epicurean dishes with a modern twist at Willington hall. The pigeon is from the surrounding woods, beetroot from a local veg shop and the pork products from the local organic farm. This dish encompasses exactly what Willington is about! Great Cheshire produce put together in a creative way. Serves 4

Ingredients

1kg raw or cooked beetroot

100g kale

25g pine nuts

25g Parmesan cheese

150ml olive oil, plus extra for cooking

300g caster sugar

150ml water

300g pork sausage meat

6 breasts of wood pigeon

4 pieces of Bury black pudding

A bunch of sage

1 sheet of all-butter puff pastry

2 eggs, beaten

Salt and freshly ground black pepper

Method

Preheat the oven to 190°C.

If you are using raw beetroot, cook it in a pan of boiling water until tender; about 1 hour. Drain and leave to cool. Take one of the beetroot and cut into medium dice and reserve for plating later. Grate the remaining beetroot.

For the kale pesto, in a hot dry pan, toast the pine nuts, taking care not to burn them. Set aside. Remove the kale leaves from the stalk and add to a food processor with the pine nuts and Parmesan. Whilst blitzing, add the oil a little at a time. Season with salt and pepper and set aside.

Prepare a sugar syrup by placing the sugar and water in pan and simmering until you have a thick consistency. Add the grated beetroot, simmer for 3 minutes, then remove from the heat and purée. Allow to cool. Place in a squeeze bottle for later.

For the sausage roll, place the sausage meat into a mixing bowl. Skin and finely dice two of the pigeon breasts and add to sausage meat. Finely dice two of the Bury black pudding pieces and add to the sausage meat mixture. Chop the sage and add it to the mixture. Season with salt and pepper and mix.

Pipe or place the mixture into a sausage shape on top of the puff pastry. Brush with beaten egg and roll into a sausage roll. Trim and brush with more of the egg wash. Bake in the preheated oven for 15-20 minutes.

Cut the remaining black pudding into the same size dice as the beetroot. Simply put the diced black pudding into the oven for the last 5 minutes of the sausage roll's cooking time.

For the pigeon, place a frying pan onto a medium heat add a little oil until it starts to smoke. Add the pigeon skin-side down and cook for 2-3 minutes on each side. Most importantly, the pigeon now needs to rest for 5 minutes. Slice each breast into three.

Have everything to hand for plating. First swirl the beetroot purée onto the plate. Add three cubes of cooked black pudding, beetroot and kale pesto. Add the warm sausage roll and the sliced pigeon.

Let the
LIQUEURS FLOW

Natural ingredients and quality produce are key to the irresistible taste of Cheshire's own hand-made liqueurs from Winding River.

Husband and wife team Matthew and Suzanne Fox fell in love with liqueurs whilst on holiday in Sorrento in 2006. The city is famous not only for its position on the stunning Amalfi Coast, but also for the irresistible lemon liqueur "limoncello".

Back in Sandbach, Cheshire, Matt and Suzanne decided to try making their own lemon liqueur, much to the delight of their family and friends who got to sample the delicious stages of recipe development. The final lemon liqueur was a hit with all who tried it, and Matt and Suzanne were encouraged to turn their hobby into a business. Lots of hard work followed. The ambitious pair embarked on a Start-up Business course at Keele University, began work on some new flavour combinations, spent months negotiating the legislation for selling alcohol and getting the correct licences in place, and eventually designed their branding. By the end of 2014, Winding River Liqueurs was ready to begin trading.

There are four core flavours available, all made using natural ingredients: lemon, strawberries and cream, orange brandy and raspberry. Whole fruits from a local supplier in Sandbach (no syrups or artificial flavourings here!) ensure only the freshest and best-quality fruits make it into their products. Winding River hand-make all their liqueurs in small batches and are always trying new ideas, which do not always include fruit. In their first year trading, they made a tea liqueur, herbal liqueur and a spiced honey whisky liqueur amongst others, all of which proved rather popular!

The liqueurs are delicious enjoyed on their own, but they are also fantastic added to a glass of Prosecco, used in cocktails or even in desserts such as crème brûlée, cheesecake or panna cotta. Seek these guys out to see what innovative liqueurs they currently have available.

Winding River Liqueurs
STRAWBERRIES AND CREAM BRULEE

Treat yourself to a boozy dessert with this delicious take on a crème brûlée.

Serves 6

Ingredients

600ml double cream

1 vanilla pod

10 medium egg yolks

4 tablespoons caster sugar, plus extra for topping

100ml Winding River Strawberries and Cream Liqueur

Method

Put six ramekins into the freezer to chill.

Put the double cream into a saucepan along with the Strawberries and Cream Liqueur. Split open the vanilla pod, scrape out the seeds and add them to the cream in the pan. Heat gently, but do not let it boil.

Place the egg yolks into a mixing bowl. Add the 4 tablespoons of caster sugar, saving the rest for later to create the crispy top. Whisk the yolks and sugar together. Just before the vanilla cream boils, add it to the yolk and sugar mixture, whisking as you pour.

Pour the mixture back in to a clean saucepan. Heat on a low to medium heat until the mixture begins to thicken. It should begin to resemble custard. Take care here that the mixture does not split. (NB If it looks like it is about to split, remove the pan from the heat and sit it in cold water, continuing to stir to cool the mixture down before returning to the heat.)

Continue to heat until the mixture becomes custard-like in thickness.

Remove the ramekins from the freezer and pour in the mixture. Put the ramekins in the fridge to cool until you are almost ready to serve the desserts.

Just prior to serving, remove the ramekins from the fridge and sprinkle a good helping of caster sugar over the top of the brûlées. If you have one, use a chef's blow torch to melt the sugar to form a crispy layer on the top of the desserts. Alternatively, set your grill to a high heat setting, sit the brûlées in a cold water bath and place under the grill until the sugar caramelises.

Welcoming YEW ALL

A place for a post-work pint at the bar, a cosy dinner in the corner or to share a bottle of wine with friends – The Yew Tree in Bunbury is a real hub of community life.

Lovingly refurbished by its owners, the Yew Tree Inn sits at the heart of Bunbury, the handsome architecture a reminder of its heritage – it was built by the Earl of Crewe in the 19th century. It's an independent family-run pub, which not only holds its own in the competitive world of Cheshire pubs, but stands head and shoulders above its rivals.

Jon and Lindsay Cox took on the pub in 2010 and slowly brought it to life, before being joined in the business by John and Helen Langley. Jon is a self-declared pub fanatic: "I would happily spend every day of my life in a pub – I just love what they mean to British society and culture." For him, a pub should be the heart of a village, somewhere to be greeted by a friendly face and a warm atmosphere.

The Yew Tree achieves just that, with the whole community coming together, from land-owners to farm hands, game-keepers to city commuters and families to young couples. It's a place for everyone to come together, feel welcome and relax. With roaring fires, flickering candles and cosy corners, it embraces the feeling of quaint British life. While in the summer, the outdoor terrace is popular for dining and drinking al fresco.

The Yew Tree is busy every night. Fifty percent of its trade comes from drinks thanks to the interesting range of real ales, craft beers, lagers, stouts and porters. The wine list is extensive and varied, as is the range of spirits.

With accolades including The Great British Pub Awards 2015 North-west Region Best Free House, the pub's popularity has extended beyond its locality. It has been named in the Good Pub Guide, The Good Food Guide, The Michelin Guide and The AA Pub Guide.

Awarded Cheshire Dining Pub of 2016 by the Good Pub Guide, The Yew Tree has a lot to shout about when it comes to its food. The focus is on quality – seasonal Cheshire produce is used where possible, with Helen's Oaklands Red Poll Beef from next door and local game a highlight in winter. Knowing the provenance of all their ingredients is key for Head Chef Rob and his Sous Chef Matt, who are given total freedom to design their menus around the finest produce.

From the ingredients to the beers and from the décor to the service, nothing is overlooked. The Yew Tree embraces all aspects of community life – it's a proper pub.

The Yew Tree

This is a popular sharing board that showcases the fantastic array of wild produce available on our doorstep. Serves 6

Ingredients

Potted Wild Rabbit:

4 wild rabbit legs (380–400g total weight)

sea salt and freshly cracked black pepper

1 tbsp sunflower oil

A large sprig of fresh thyme

2 bay leaves

2 cloves garlic, crushed

1 litre chicken stock

7 tbsp goose fat, melted

2 banana shallots, finely diced

1 tsp finely chopped fresh thyme leaves

1 tbsp finely chopped gherkins

1 tbsp finely chopped capers

6 drops of Tabasco sauce

½ tsp Worcestershire sauce

Venison Scotch Eggs:

3 eggs

300g venison sausages

2 tbsp finely chopped fresh mixed soft herbs (such as parsley, chervil and chives)

1 tbsp plain flour, seasoned with salt and pepper

1–2 eggs, lightly beaten

150g fresh breadcrumbs or Panko breadcrumbs

sunflower oil, for deep-frying

Walnut and Raisin Beer Bread:

1 pint Stonehouse Station bitter

500g self-raising flour

60g raisins

15 walnuts

2 tbsp caster sugar

Method

To prepare the potted wild rabbit, preheat the oven to 160°C. Season the rabbit legs with sea salt and freshly cracked black pepper. Heat the sunflower oil in a casserole dish until hot, then add the seasoned rabbit legs and cook over a high heat for 3 minutes on each side or until golden brown. Add the sprig of fresh thyme, bay leaves, 1 clove of crushed garlic and stock. Bring the stock to the boil and boil for 4 minutes, then remove from the heat. Cover the pan with a lid, then transfer to the oven and cook for about 1 hour or until the rabbit is tender. Remove from the oven and leave to cool in the stock for 30 minutes.

While the rabbit is cooling, heat 1 tbsp of the goose fat in a small saucepan. Add the diced banana shallots and the other clove of crushed garlic, then cover the pan and sweat over a low heat for 8–10 minutes or until soft and transparent. Remove from the heat. Drain the rabbit legs, reserving the stock. Flake the rabbit meat into a mixing bowl (discard the bones). Add the cooked shallots, thyme, chopped gherkins, finely chopped capers, Tabasco sauce, Worcestershire sauce, 3 tablespoons melted goose fat and salt and pepper and mix well. Divide the mixture evenly between six small glass serving jars, packing it in well using the back of a spoon. Chill in the fridge for 30 minutes. Melt 3 tablespoons goose fat and pour it on top of the chilled rabbit mixture, dividing it evenly between the jars. Return the potted rabbit to the fridge for a further 30 minutes before serving.

Next prepare the venison Scotch eggs. Cook the eggs in a covered saucepan of boiling water for 6 minutes, then remove the eggs using a slotted spoon and place them in a bowl of iced water to cool them quickly. Once cold, peel the eggs carefully. Meanwhile, remove the skins from the venison sausages, place the sausage meat in a bowl with the herbs and mix well. Divide and shape the mixture into 3 equal balls. Press each ball of venison mixture flat, place a peeled boiled egg in the centre of each one and then wrap the venison mixture around the egg, enclosing each egg completely. Place the balls on a plate and chill in the fridge for 10 minutes.

Put the seasoned flour, beaten eggs and breadcrumbs into 3 separate shallow bowls. First, roll a venison-covered egg in the seasoned flour, tapping off the excess flour, then roll it in the beaten egg and then finally in the breadcrumbs, making sure it is evenly coated all over. Repeat this process with the other 2 venison-covered eggs. Return to the plate and chill in the fridge for 15–20 minutes to rest and firm up. Using a deep fryer or a heated deep pan of sunflower oil heated to 180°C, fry the Scotch eggs until golden before placing on a baking tray and into the heated oven for 6-7 minutes.

For the beer bread, preheat the oven to 185°C. Add 500ml of the Stonehouse Station bitter to the self-raising flour. Soak the raisins in the remaining beer and add sugar, seasoning, walnuts and drained soaked raisins to beer and flour mix. Pour into a greased loaf tin. Cook for 25 minutes.

From Yu TO YOU

The talented Yu brothers are taking modern Chinese cuisine to the next level in their new restaurant, Yu Alderley Edge.

Cooking has been in the Yu family for decades, and for brothers Victor and Vinny, working alongside their father Charlie has been an inspirational culinary journey. They decided it was time to take everything they had learnt from their talented father and combine them with the new skills and techniques they have acquired from their collaborations with other chefs and from their travels around the world.

The natural evolution to starting their own restaurant took careful consideration, as they had to find the right site for the vision they had in mind – something new and distinctive. Alderley Edge, with its thriving food scene and plethora of adventurous diners, was the perfect place to launch their dynamic style of contemporary Chinese cooking.

Head Chef Victor uses the best ingredients and a mixture of traditional and modern methods to create his unique menu. His aim, along with brother Vinny who manages the front of house team, was to raise the bar in Chinese cuisine. They hope that people will have their eyes opened to the wonderful range of dishes on offer and the variety of cooking styles that

are used – and diners are being blown away by the fresh, light and fragrant dishes on offer. For many who dine here, it completely changes their preconceptions of what Chinese food is about.

The chic and sophisticated interior has been carefully considered, and it is the ideal setting for the stunningly creative dishes that come out of the kitchen. The luxurious feel of the interior is a stylish mix of traditional Chinese features and sophisticated modern style. The bar, where guests can enjoy a cocktail before dinner is an elegant meeting place – in fact many people come just to enjoy one of their signature cocktails and some dim sum at the bar.

Whether it's a post-work cocktail, an intimate dinner for two or a large gathering, Yu aims to provide the ultimate setting and bespoke banquet, complemented by excellent wine and exceptional service for an unforgettable experience.

Yu Alderley Edge
VICTOR'S SIGNATURE STEAMED SEA BASS, SPRING ONION, CHILLI AND GINGER

You will need a steam oven, electric steamer or a saucepan with steamer basket to make Victor's famous signature sea bass dish. Serves 2

Ingredients

2 sea bass fillets, 125g each, skin left on

20g ginger, peeled

2 spring onions, green tops only

½ red chilli, seeds removed

A drizzle of rapeseed oil

Sauce:

1 tbsp soya sauce

1 tbsp rice wine

1 tsp sesame oil

1 tsp caster sugar

1 tbsp water

Method

If you're using a steam oven, preheat it to 200°C with 100% humidity. Alternatively, if you're using an electric steamer, preheat it following the manufacturer's instructions or place a saucepan over a high heat, fill two-thirds with water and bring to the boil. Fit the steamer basket on top of the saucepan and reduce to a simmer.

Inspect the fish for pin bones and trim off any fat. Cut the fish fillets into three equal pieces each and place in an ovenproof dish.

Use a sharp knife to slice the vegetables into fine julienne and place half in a bowl. Set the other half of the vegetables aside.

Heat a little rapeseed oil in a small saucepan and, when hot, pour into the bowl. Toss the ginger, spring onions and chilli into the hot oil using a spoon and then pour over the fish. Use your hands to coat the fish well in the oil and then place skin-side down into the ovenproof dish.

Top the fish with the remaining julienne of vegetables and place in the steamer. Steam for 3 minutes.

In the meantime, make the sauce by placing all the ingredients in a small pan and bring to the boil. Remove from the heat.

To serve, arrange the fish in a row in the centre of a warmed plate, with some pieces showing the skin, other pieces the flesh. Top with the julienne of vegetables and spoon some of the sauce around. Serve immediately.

WOK-SEARED WAGYU BEEF WITH SWEET SOYA, LIME, GINGER AND CHILLI

This dish has so many great memories for me. I believe in using great produce with simple cooking methods to end up with the best possible results. Such methods have been passed on to me from my father, which he has collected during his 50-year culinary journey. Serves 4

Ingredients

170g wagyu fillet or 21-day rib-eye beef

100ml dark soya sauce

50ml fresh lime juice

50ml honey

1 garlic clove

Ginger

Chilli

1 tbsp vegetable oil

1 tbsp rice wine

1 tsp cornflour, if needed

Steamed rice, to serve

Method

Trim and cut the wagyu beef into 1cm cubes.

Infuse the soya sauce, lime juice and honey together. Set aside. Slice the garlic, ginger and half a chilli into strips.

Heat a wok with the vegetable oil. Sear the wagyu beef on each side and leave to rest. Now add the garlic, ginger, chilli and rice wine and deglaze.

Add the wagyu beef back into the wok plus 4-5 tbsp of the soya mixture. Stir-fry together for 3-5 minutes, depending on how rare you would like your beef. Add the cornflour if needed to thicken the sauce. Serve with steamed rice.

The DIRECTORY

These great businesses have supported the making of this book; please support and enjoy them.

Bents Garden & Home
Warrington Road
Glazebury, Warrington
Cheshire WA3 5NT
Telephone: 01942 266300
Website: www.bents.co.uk
Discover a destination with a difference at Bents Garden & Home with family-friendly attractions, an inspirational shopping environment and a choice of dining destinations.

Big 5 Catering
NoWFOOD Centre, University of Chester
Parkgate Road
Chester CH1 4AR
Telephone:
01244 511457 / 0783 4488 124
Website: www.big5catering.co.uk
Twitter: @big5catering
Facebook: www.facebook.com/big5catering
Hog Roast, Lamb Spit Roast and South African BBQ (Braai) Specialists.

The Brew Foundation
Telephone: 07803 719797
Website: www.theBrewFoundation.co.uk
Email: sales@thebrewfoundation.co.uk
Facebook: www.facebook.com/BrewFoundation
Twitter: @BrewFoundation
Craft micro-brewery run by a father and son team where drinkability is key.

Cheerbrook Farm Shop
Newcastle Road, Nantwich
Cheshire CW5 7EL
Telephone: 01270 666431
Website: www.cheerbrook.co.uk
Award-winning, family-run farm shop and café providing top-quality, great-value, local food with excellent customer service.

The Chef's Table
4 Music Hall Passage
Chester CH1 2EU
Telephone: 01244 403040
Website: www.chefstablechester.co.uk
Award-winning restaurant in the centre of Chester, famous for creating its menus weekly around the very best seasonal produce available.

The Chester Fields
Sandfield Farm
Chester Road
Chester CH2 4JR
Telephone: 01244 303100
Website: www.thechesterfields.co.uk
A stunning country pub and restaurant set in the heart of the Cheshire countryside yet only 4 miles from Chester city centre.

Chester Town Criers
Julie & David Mitchell
6 Panton Place, Hoole
Chester CH2 3JE
Telephone: 01244 311736
Website: www.chestertowncriers.com
Town criers, costumed after-dinner speakers and much more.

Chime Hartford
279 Chester Road
Hartford, Northwich
Cheshire CW8 1QL
Telephone: 01606 872158
Website: www.chimehartford.co.uk
A chic restaurant set in the Cheshire countryside with fantastic wines and fabulous cocktails.

The Clink Restaurant
HMP Styal, Wilmslow
Cheshire East SK9 4HR
Telephone: 01625 553146
Website: www.theclinkcharity.org
The Clink Restaurant transforms the lives of the women prisoners working there through work-based training and education, whilst serving seasonal dishes that are created using fresh and locally-sourced produce.

DeFINE Food & Wine
2 School Lane, Sandiway
Northwich CW8 2NH
Telephone: 01606 882101
Website: www.definefoodandwine.com
One of the country's leading independent wine merchants and delicatessens.

Deli-vert
10a Faulkner Street
Hoole, Chester CH2 3BD
Telephone: 01244 340505
Website: www.deli-vert.co.uk
Chester-based delicatessen bringing together fine foods from Cheshire and beyond

The Egerton Arms
Knutsford Road
Chelford, Macclesfield
Cheshire SK11 9BB
Telephone: 01625 861366
Website: www.chelfordegertonarms.co.uk
A traditional family-run country pub, serving real ales and quality, locally-sourced food.

The Fat Loaf
62 Green Lane
Ashton-On-Mersey, Sale
Cheshire M33 5PG
Telephone: 0161 972 0397
Website: www.thefatloaf.co.uk
Twitter: @thefatloafsale
We are a bistro cooking fresh food that's affordable enough to be a week day habit and special enough for a weekend treat!

The Garden
154 Ashley Road, Hale
Cheshire WA15 9SA
Telephone: 0161 941 6702
Website: www.thegardenhale.co.uk
Twitter: @thegardenhale
Facebook: www.facebook.com/thegardenhale
Organic café serving earth-friendly food with a focus on local, seasonal produce.

Great North Pie Co.
2A Deanway, Manchester Road
Wilmslow, Cheshire SK9 3HW
Telephone: 01625 522112
Website: www.greatnorthpie.co
Artisan pie makers and Supreme Champion of the British Pie Awards 2015.

The Hanging Gate
Higher Sutton
Macclesfield
Cheshire SK11 0NG
Telephone: 01260 400756
Website: www.thehanginggate.co.uk
Stunning destination pub offering fantastic homemade food, exceptionally well-kept real ales and breath-taking views.

Harthill Cookery School and Terrace
The Green
Harthill, nr Chester
Cheshire CH3 9LQ
Telephone: 01829 782097
Website: www.brianmellor.co.uk
Award-winning cookery school in a stunning rural setting featuring indoor and outdoor cookery courses.

H.E. Coward Traditional Butchers and Bakery
68A Main Street, Frodsham
Cheshire WA6 7AU
Telephone: 01928 733233
Website: www.hecoward.co.uk
Facebook: www.facebook.com / HEcoward
Twitter: @cowardsbutchers
A traditional family-run butchers since 1929. Proudly serving our customers with 100% British meat and finest quality pies.

The Hollies Farm Shops
Website: www.theholliesfarmshop.co.uk
Little Budworth
Tarporley Road, Little Budworth
Cheshire CW6 9ES
Telephone: 01829 760414
Lower Stretton
Walnut Tree Farm, Northwich Road
Lower Stretton WA4 4PG
Telephone: 01925 730976
Award-winning farm shops, coffee shops, butcheries, deli, gift barns and forest lodges. A family business, four generations in the making – the family's passion lies in sourcing great food and providing the best customer service through every part of the business.

International Cheese Awards
The Woodlands
Aston, Nantwich
Cheshire CW5 8DB
Telephone: 01270 780306
Website: www.
internationalcheeseawards.co.uk
*Nantwich Show is home of the
International Cheese Awards. Set in the
beautiful South Cheshire countryside, just
one mile from Nantwich Town Centre at
the historic stately home Dorfold Hall.*

Jones Deli @ The Egerton Arms
Knutsford Road
Chelford, Macclesfield
Cheshire SK11 9BB
Telephone: 01625 860900
Website: www.jonesdeli.co.uk
*A new and exciting Cheshire deli selling
the finest local and artisan produce,
annexed to the Egerton Arms pub in
Chelford Village.*

Joseph Benjamin Restaurant
134-138 Northgate Street
Chester CH1 2HT
Telephone: 01244 344295
Website: www.josephbenjamin.co.uk
*One of Chester's most popular
independent restaurants, Joseph
Benjamin is run by two brothers and
made its name providing exceptional
quality food and impeccable service in an
un-fussy, unpretentious style.*

Kenyon Hall Farm
Winwick Lane, Croft
Warrington WA3 7ED
Telephone: 01925 763646
Website: www.kenyonhall.co.uk
Delivery business: www.
northernharvest.co.uk
*Set in the Cheshire countryside is the
family-run Kenyon Hall Farm Shop, Café,
Plant Centre and 'Pick Your Own' fields.*

The Little Deli Company
42 Stamford Park Road
Hale WA15 9EP
Telephone: 07955 619635
Website: www.thelittledelicompany.
co.uk
Twitter: @thelittledelico
Facebook: Thelittledelicompany
*Working with independent local farmers
and producers, as well as specialist
Continental farmers and food importers,
The Little Deli Company aims to provide
a one-stop shop for food lovers.*

The Lord Clyde
36 Clarke Lane
Kerridge, Bollington
Cheshire SK10 5AH
Telephone: 01625 562123
Website: www.thelordclyde.co.uk
*A cosy gastro pub celebrating the
wondrous tastes of each season in the
lovely village of Kerridge.*

Mrs Darlington's Preserves
Darlington & Daughters
Lancaster Fields, Crewe
Cheshire CW16FF
Telephone: 01270 250710
Website: www.mrsdarlingtons.com
Mrs Darlington's Preserves, Cheshire
– Producer of award-winning and
homemade tasting curds, preserves,
chutneys and condiments.

My Secret Feasts
Locations throughout Cheshire and
North Wales
Telephone: 07540 970226
Facebook: www.facebook.com/
mysecretfeasts
Twitter: @mysecretfeasts
*A pop up dining experience in unique
locations – join in one of our evenings or
gather your own clan together.*

Orsom Handmade Cheese
Laurels Farm, Crewe Road
Hatherton, Nantwich
Cheshire CW5 7PE
Telephone: 01270 841500
*Website: www.orsomcheese.co.uk
Handmade cheese with a touch of
personality, Orsom brings something new
to the table.*

Piste Wine Bar & Restaurant
55 High St, Tarporley
Cheshire CW6 0DP
Telephone: 01829 732483
Website: www.pistetarporley.com
*A family-run wine bar and restaurant
with an informal, relaxed 'Alpine chic'
atmosphere.*

Porta Tapas
140 Northgate Street
Chester CH1 2HT
No Phone (No Reservations!)
Website: www.portatapas.co.uk
*From the team behind Joseph Benjamin
Restaurant comes this award-winning
pint-sized tapas bar beneath Chester's
historic walls.*

Residence Restaurant & Bar
9 Mill Street, Nantwich
Cheshire CW5 5ST
Telephone: 01270 629100
Website: www.residence.uk.com
*Residence Restaurant & Bar has been
independently owned since 2007 and has
truly established itself as an award-
winning venue with fine food, great
cocktails and superb service.*

Rolando's
18 The Cross
Lymm WA13 0HU
Telephone: 01925 756067
Website: www.rolandoslymm.com
*Independent family-owned Italian
eatery.*

The Salt Bar
23b Church Street
Macclesfield SK11 6LB
Telephone: 01625 432221
Website: www.thesaltbar.co.uk
A Scandinavian restaurant serving simple quality food in an intimate and cosy atmosphere on the historic cobbles of Macclesfield, with three boutique bed and breakfast rooms above.

Simon Radley at The Chester Grosvenor
The Chester Grosvenor
56-58 Eastgate Street
Chester, CH1 1LT
Telephone: 01244 895618
Website: www.ChesterGrosvenor.com
Simon Radley at The Chester Grosvenor offers contemporary dining in an atmosphere of chic sophistication. The award-winning restaurant has retained its Michelin star since 1990, has four AA rosettes and has been recognised as one of the top 100 restaurants in the UK by The Sunday Times. The restaurant was also crowned Best Hotel Restaurant at the European Hospitality Awards 2015.

Stockyard
106-108 Ashley Road
Hale, WA14 2UN
Telephone: 0161 928 2343
Website: www.stockyardhale.co.uk
Twitter: @StockyardHale
Facebook: www.facebook.com/stockyardhale
BBQ & liquor – burgers, hot dogs, grills, gumbo, lobster and bbq meats from the smoker.

Sugo Pasta Kitchen
22 Shaw's Rd, Altrincham
Cheshire WA14 1QU
Telephone: 0161 929 7706
Website: www.sugopastakitchen.co.uk
Manchester's first pasta restaurant dedicated to regional southern Italian cooking.

Taste Cheshire
West Wing Offices,
Chester Railway Station
Station Road, Chester CH1 3NT
Telephone: 01244 405610
Website: www.tastecheshire.com
Connecting people with a real taste of Cheshire.

Walk Mill
Walk Mill Lane
Waverton, Chester
Cheshire CH3 7BF
Telephone: 01829 749373
Water mill stone-grinding home-grown wheat to make flour, which is used to bake goods for the on-site cafe and sold for wholesale and retail.

Willington Hall Hotel
Willington, Tarporley
Chester CW6 0NB
Telephone: 01829 752321
Website: www.willingtonhall.co.uk
A twelve-bedded country house hotel in rural Cheshire, serving British food with a modern twist.

Winding River Liqueurs Limited
Sandbach, Cheshire
Telephone:
07971 897368 / 07789 917162
Email:
windingriverliqueurs@hotmail.com
Facebook: www.facebook.com/windingriverliqueurs
Twitter: @WinRivLiqueurs
Winding River Liqueurs use natural ingredients to create exciting recipes and taste combinations.

The Yew Tree Inn
Long Lane
Spurstow, Bunbury
Cheshire CW6 9RD
Telephone: 01829 260274
Website: www.theyewtreebunbury.com
Village pub serving freshly made, locally-sourced food combined with informal service in a cosy and relaxed atmosphere.

Yu Alderley Edge
London Road, Alderley Edge
Cheshire SK9 7QD
Telephone: 01625 569922
Website: www.yualderleyedge.com
Yu prides itself on providing a distinctive, contemporary take on traditional Chinese cuisine, sourcing the best ingredients to create exceptional dishes.